Successful Job Hunting

# Successful Job Hunting

## for Managers, Professionals and Graduates

R. C. I. Miller

Basil Blackwell

© R. C. I. Miller 1983

First published 1983

Reprinted 1984, 1986

Second edition 1988

Basil Blackwell Ltd
108 Cowley Road, Oxford OX4 1JF, UK

Basil Blackwell Inc.
432 Park Avenue South, Suite 1503,
New York, NY 10015, USA

All rights reserved. No part of this publication may be reproduced, stored in a retrieval system, or transmitted, in any form or by any means, electronic, mechanical, photocopying, recording or otherwise, without the prior permission of the publisher.

Except in the United States of America, this book is sold subject to the condition that it shall not, by way of trade or otherwise, be lent, re-sold, hired out, or otherwise circulated without the publisher's prior consent in any form of binding or cover other than that in which it is published and without a similar condition including this condition being imposed on the subsequent purchaser.

*British Library Cataloguing in Publication Data*

Miller, R. C. I. (Ron C. I.)
   Successful job hunting : for managers, professionals
   and graduates – 2nd ed.
   1. Job hunting – Manuals – For executives
   I. Title
   650.1′4
ISBN 0-631-16453-7

Typesetting by Getset (BTS) Ltd, Eynsham, Oxford.
Printed in Great Britain by Billing and Sons, Worcester.

# Contents

| | | |
|---|---|---|
| | *Introduction* | 1 |
| 1 | Why People Work | 4 |
| 2 | Building a Résumé | 9 |
| 3 | Locating Employers and Jobs | 31 |
| 4 | Dealing with Application Forms and Tests | 49 |
| 5 | Preparation for the Interview | 57 |
| 6 | The Interview | 74 |
| 7 | After the Interview | 93 |
| 8 | Self-employed – or unemployed? | 98 |
| 9 | From College to Career | 104 |
| 10 | Action Plan | 121 |
| | *The Seven Point Plan* | 124 |
| | *Useful Publications and Addresses* | 126 |
| | *Index* | 130 |

To Douglas, Stuart and Karen.
With thanks to Pauline for help and advice.

# Introduction

This book is written to help people who want to make career progress. It is intended for those in professional or managerial posts, and will also be useful to graduating students, as the strategies explained are designed to help all applicants present themselves in the best possible way. Chapter 9 deals specifically with the position of the college leaver.

The advice I offer reflects the fact that in today's depressed economy, competition for a job begins when the applicant first makes contact with the prospective employer. If it is to stand out from hundreds of other applications, that initial approach must be right – there will be no second chance. Employers must be convinced that they want to meet the person behind the written words – otherwise there will be no job. You may be brilliant and charming, but if you don't even reach the interview no one will find this out. Today's problem, different from yesterday's, is to clear the first hurdle and get that vital invitation to an interview. I have therefore concentrated in the first few chapters on this stage; if you follow the advice given you stand a much greater chance of obtaining interviews than your competitors.

Interview technique is considered in chapters 5, 6 and 9, which give guidance sufficient for the needs of most job hunters. Remember that it is the *approach* that should be followed, not always the exact details. Never 'learn' answers to possible interview questions before you go, and always observe carefully what kind of person or organization you are dealing with and match your response to them.

For the unemployed, job hunting is a specially tough and lonely task. Stripped of colleagues, facilities and in all likelihood some self-confidence, unemployed job hunters must apply themselves totally to the quest for work, and they need all the support they can get from friends and family. When the breadwinner is out of work, all members of the family will have to learn that funds and tempers will be short, resisting the temptation to blame anyone for their situation. The former breadwinner will be around the house all day, most days, and other members of the family must try to be supportive and patient. Loyalty and understanding are essential. It is in the whole family's long-term interests to present a united front – the family which breaks under the strain only brings extra problems to all its members then and in the future.

Single people will find that their time is filled with job hunting, particularly in the early weeks, as well as the normal household tasks. If there is time to spare, try to do additional background reading to prevent the danger of boredom or laziness taking over.

For students, success in finding the right opportunity now may make all the difference between a career and a succession of jobs. Women at all stages in a career can find extra problems in convincing prospective employers that they are capable and likely to have a continuing commitment to the job. This issue is tackled in chapter 5.

Successful job hunting requires commitment and hard work. Luck is not to be scorned, but it is no substitute for effort and self-motivation. I have tried to outline in this book an approach which, if adopted wholeheartedly, will improve your chances of getting a job. I do not attempt to cover the specific situation which applies in every trade or profession, because the job-obtaining process is similar throughout – initial written application followed by one or two interviews.

My examples tend to come from industry, because that environment is recognized and understood by the majority of people, but the method adopted is equally applicable across the board.

# 1

# Why People Work

Society exerts many unwritten but all-powerful constraints over individuals. As with any set of rules, there are always plenty of people who choose to break them, but the overwhelming majority are expected to conform. To work for a living is the norm expected by society; it thus comes as a tremendous shock when events conspire to destroy one of our basic expectations which has previously been taken for granted – a belief that there will be work for all who want it.

Britain is not unique in experiencing severe unemployment; the problem stems at least partly from the worldwide recession which began in the early 1970s. It has affected all nations to some degree, but the problems in the United Kingdom have been exacerbated by a shake-out of jobs which have existed for many years – or which were thought to exist. This over-manning is no longer tolerated, as British industry fights for survival against the rest of the trading world, and so people who thought they had jobs for life now find themselves competing for the reduced number of jobs which are available.

With the economy recovered from the trough, the new problem is technology – fewer people are needed to produce more goods. Although new jobs are appearing, it is likely that there will be a surplus of people over vacancies with the resultant unemployment flattening out at a higher level than would have been considered tolerable only a few years ago. No one wants to see anyone who wants a job unemployed but the fact remains that some people will be unemployed, and so the fight for jobs remains a tough one.

## WHO NEEDS WORK?

Why do we want work? Why is it important to us to have a job? There are a number of valid reasons.

Work gives the individual a sense of purpose. Knowing that he is expected to make an agreed number of calls each day, the salesman keeps pushing on. The designer understands that her project has to be ready within a certain time. The bus driver is required to complete his daily route. Let all these people report for work but give them no set tasks and, after the first few days while the novelty lasts, they will all lose that sense of purpose which they previously experienced. Take away the job altogether and the loss is greater still.

People work for self-respect. We derive part of our identity from what we do, and unemployment can leave us without an answer to the question 'What are you?'.

Employment brings friends and companionship. Being cut off from them on retirement can cause old people to lose interest in life, which in turn may bring premature death. Younger people who lose their jobs are luckier as they are usually fitter, both mentally and physically, and often have other sources of friends. Even so, there is unlikely to be a satisfactory substitute for workmates.

Unless we are among the very few who inherit wealth or win the pools, work means money. Without a wage or salary, we are dependent on benefits distributed by the state and paid for by those in work. The simple arithmetic of benefits, allowances, taxes and population means that we need an income if we are to raise our standards of living above the most basic level.

## MOVING ON

Whatever job we have, our objectives are being met to some extent. But people change jobs because they want a better one – 'better' meaning different things to different people.

People move on for a variety of reasons. Some want more money, some seek to escape personality conflicts, some want to move to a more attractive area and some want better working conditions. Others pursue promotion or decide to change course completely. Those who seek a career rather than simply a job will want to make progress for one or more of the above reasons. Some will achieve all they need in one company, but the days of fifty years with one firm are over. Anyone who has been with the same company for over ten years risks being seen by employers as lacking initiative and drive. Long service can be a distinct handicap when the time does come for a move. Most people will move at least five or six times in their working lives.

There are many reasons for this change: better education, communications and travel have all contributed and, on occasion, the pressures of inflation have encouraged more people to look around. A typical career pattern now shows that the average period spent in any one job is just over six years, with longer service in the second half of a career as pension rights become part of the decision to move or stay. But new arrangements in that area will soon begin to affect length of service. In the USA, the average time with a company is already down to around four years, and Britain will probably follow in due course.

Job changing is here to stay, and while some people are concerned at the rate at which it occurs, it does bring advantages. People bring new skills to a job and, at the same time, learn from their new colleagues. That helps to raise standards and new products, companies and even industries emerge.

## COMPETITION FOR JOBS

Redundancy has brought many more people into the job market, albeit unwillingly. Unemployment, unless it is a chosen way of life, is no longer the social stigma which it once was, and those unfortunate enough to have been thrown out of work are competing with people who are employed but want to move on. To find any job or to find a better job is now much tougher than at any time in the last fifty years. Men and women who suffered in the depression of the 1920s and 1930s are now retired and an entirely new generation is facing an old problem.

The job shortage is especially strange to the student world. Higher education facilities were expanded at a rapid rate from the early 1960s onwards in order to turn out more graduates. In the early 1970s, employers were vying with each other on the annual recruitment interviews at colleges and universities (the 'milk round') to sign up the pick of the crop. Now many major companies are visiting only a handful of campuses. They find it impossible to take on new recruits while at the same time cutting back on experienced staff who are already trained and contributing to the company. For the first year or two, graduates cost firms more than they give back in value and so, with a drastically reduced number of openings, the graduate's battle for a place on the ladder is as tough as anyone else's.

All job hunters need to review their skills and knowledge and then sell them. It is useless to be the best out-of-work designer if you cannot find somewhere to sell and utilize your talent. If you are out of work you must put aside your professional knowledge for a while and learn how to find work and then how to use your new skills to land a job. People in work must take a similar view if they are to promote their careers and achieve the best financial rewards.

Job changing is more competitive than ever before. It cannot be emphasized too strongly that old job skills count for little; job-hunting ability is what is all important. Failure to recognize the need to acquire that skill will mean stagnation or long-term unemployment. When the talk is of high unemployment, the fact that there are scores of vacancies waiting for the right candidates to fill them is often overlooked. The figures hide the fact that the unemployment total is not a fixed mass of humanity but at least partly a fast-changing number of people who enter and leave the list daily.

Competition for vacancies in job-hunting is unusual in that the candidates rarely see each other. Because of this, many job hunters act as if there is no competition, approaching the task with less drive than they would show in an open contest. It is also hard to think of any other quest for victory where the adversaries rely more on their past than on their present and future. Imagine the FA Cup being won on the basis of competing clubs' past records instead of out on the field! Yet many job applicants think in these terms.

Only a few people seem to understand that jobs are only won by those who *appear* best qualified. Those who *are* best qualified may not even be interviewed, and will certainly not be appointed if they do not even get as far as meeting their potential employer.

# 2
# Building a Résumé

## HOW NOT TO BEGIN

Most job hunters, perhaps as many as 95 per cent, fail to consider the essentials of presenting themselves attractively in a buyers' market. The first thing most of them do is write a curriculum vitae or career history which invariably takes the form of a list of schools, colleges, employers and dates, perhaps with job titles being added for good measure. Résumés of that type belong in an obituary column and are just about as interesting to the potential employer. The job hunter's next step might be to borrow a typewriter, tap out this information and then have fifty or so photocopies made of the result. The total outlay would probably not exceed £5.

If the same people were trying to sell their house or car, would they consider it a good sales point to list all the previous owners and their dates of ownership? Would they not expect to spend some money making the item look its best and then marketing it in as attractive a way as possible? Would they not emphasize its good points? These seem such obvious steps to take when we are selling valuable items, but when it comes to promoting a career worth perhaps half a million pounds, we accept lower standards. Any expenditure over £10 is considered extravagant, and even the purchase price of this book will have been the subject of second or third thoughts for many readers!

Our traditional job hunters, now armed with copies of their career histories, then compound their folly. They answer a few advertisements, scan the Yellow Pages and send off résumés to the various employment agencies they have found, passing the odd copy of the c.v. to influential friends and even applying to the occasional box number. After doing all that for a month or two and achieving no success, our job hunters become frustrated but believe they are doing all they can to find a better job.

They have in fact failed completely to understand the size of the problem and the odds against succeeding with such a disorganized approach. Unless our job hunters learn that they have to market themselves, they will remain among the 95 per cent who never discover the secrets of successful job hunting.

**FIRST STEPS**

Successful job hunting depends on good planning and lots of spade work. Attention to detail now will save problems later, and I have noted the major points for action below.

Attitude of mind is all important. When there is a shortage of jobs, many people genuinely think that there are no good jobs available. If you, the job hunter, are to be successful, you must develop an optimistic view just as you would in other aspects of life. To apply for a job with the feeling that your application will fail is certain to bring about that result, as your defeatism will show through.

Optimism can easily give way to pessimism when months pass and success remains elusive. Using a rule of thumb to estimate the time-scale will help you to avoid depression, as you will have a better idea of what lies ahead. In a typical case, with unemployment around 10 per cent, to find a job will take one month for every £1,000 of salary expected although there will be wide variations around the average depending on the skills you can offer and the demand for them.

Avoid pessimism by changing your approach completely; that in itself can raise your morale.

## SETTING YOUR SIGHTS

The people who succeed in life are those who have clear objectives. After all, it is undeniably best to decide on a destination before planning a route, although there is nothing wrong with checking the map at some stage and making a detour.

Serious job hunters should think about the reasons why they want to move and make a list. This will be less than complete if it has fewer than twenty or so items in it and, as a starting point, these might include:

| | |
|---|---|
| new location | better working conditions |
| more involvement with people | more money |
| greater security | new career field |
| new colleagues | more involvement with policy |
| more physical work | more mental work |
| more travel | less travel |
| greater status | more challenge |
| more teamwork | more independence |
| regular hours | variable hours |
| preference for bigger firm | preference for smaller firm |
| family needs or partner's move | skills now redundant |
| contracting industry | promotion prospects |

The list is unlikely to be completed at one sitting. Once it is finished, you need to think about your priorities. We all have our own ideas, but it is essential to accept that not everything can be top priority and only by identifying what really matters can you focus your planning. Then it is time to consider the industries and types of work which are most likely to satisfy your career ambitions.

Skill and experience must be taken into account, but do not let them prevent your making a wide-ranging self-examination which may point to a need for some retraining before you can achieve the desired change of direction. If your financial situation precludes time out for retraining (as is likely), some compromise will be needed, but there is no harm in recognizing the point. It may also be the time to look into other ways of acquiring new skills; evening classes might provide an answer.

Most graduates have some preferences for their future careers and, if they have received good advice and have acted on it, their studies and qualifications will have been aimed at their ultimate choice of career. It is obvious that firms which are fighting to survive will be more attracted to graduates whose interests relate closely to their needs than to those from the more academic and less marketable courses of study. Today's graduates, if they want to make an early start on their careers, must expect to have to come down to earth and face the realities of life more quickly than their predecessors of ten or twenty years ago.

## THE UNEMPLOYED DILEMMA

The list of reasons which a person might have for wanting a move apply equally, in the longer term, to someone who is unemployed; in the short term, however, unemployed job hunters may find themselves facing a dilemma – to stick out for what they regard as career progress or to take a job at a lower level just to get back into work. The arguments for taking *any* job are strong, not least to avoid the mutterings of the neighbours who will wonder why such a well-qualified person is unable to find anything. A job also brings in money above the unemployment benefit level, restores morale and allows job hunters to avoid the label of 'unemployed' when they apply for the next job in their career plan.

Against these arguments is the problem that being at work automatically makes it harder to be available for interviews and there is a risk that future employers will criticize the fact that you failed to keep your place on the ladder – were you just not good enough and had to climb down a rung? If there is some truth in that, are you really fit to return to and improve upon your old level?

Unemployed job hunters will quickly find that there are very few companies who will even consider employing someone who previously earned more than they plan to pay to fill their vacancy. Employers know perfectly well that you are not likely to stay a moment longer than it takes you to find something better, when they will have the cost and inconvenience of filling the post all over again. They also know that while you remain you will want more time off to attend interviews so that their needs will not be met. There is even the chance that job hunters will be better able to do their bosses' job than they themselves can – which causes its own set of problems for the company.

All in all, trying to find work at a lower level than before is not as simple as you might expect and, not surprisingly, it brings as many problems as it solves. Job hunters must think very hard about their own circumstances before jumping to the obvious conclusion that any work is better than none.

One answer to the problem can be to sign up with some organization such as Executive Standby or Executive Manpower Services. Local self-help organizations are forming in many towns and can be contacted through Jobcentres or PER (Professional and Executive Recruitment). They may be able to offer temporary jobs for redundant executives who want to earn a few pounds by working in local companies which need occasional expert help. (But note that entitlement to Unemployment Benefit may be affected depending on the hours and fees involved – check with the Jobcentre to avoid breaking the rules.) These self-help groups are also useful in bringing together professionals from various disciplines whose skills can complement each other in the search for permanent new appointments.

It is possible that, despite following the advice offered in this book, some readers might find themselves out of work for six months or more. If that misfortune should befall you for whatever reason then, courtesy of the taxpayer, you have some extra help on tap.

This comes in the form of a Job Club which is an organization run and paid for by the Department of Employment through the Jobcentres. So far, they are only open to anyone who has been out of work for six months or more but, given that unwanted qualification, anyone can join. That tends to mean that the typical Job Club will have a majority of members coming from the unqualified job hunters although their need for a job is just as great as anyone else's. The mix will vary according to the town in which the Club operates (and many towns have more than one Club).

So what do the Clubs offer? They will train members how to apply for jobs, help them to complete a CV and give them advice on applying for jobs and being interviewed. Many professional people, especially those who have read and used the approach in this book, will consider this unnecessary but there is nothing wrong in listening to and using other people's ideas and then selecting those points which are most relevant to your needs. One of the greatest benefits of the Job Club is that it provides free use of the telephone, and free stationary and stamps as well as typing and copying facilities – valuable support when funds might be low.

The facilities are available on one condition – the job hunter must make at least 10 'contacts' per day by letter and/or telephone to people or firms who might be able, directly or indirectly, to hold out the prospect of a job. It is a modest price for generous help.

Job Clubs are usually limited to about 15 people in each group for the sessions in which training in job hunting is given, thus allowing individual help to be given. The training takes place for four half days per week for two weeks, then there is unlimited access to the phones etc., provided the minimum number of contacts are made. About two-thirds of Job Club members find jobs within ten weeks, the remainder tending to quit before then.

Without in any way criticising the system, because experience shows that knowing the rudiments of Job Hunting is limited to the minority of job hunters, the fact remains that Club members are taught a standard approach which, amongst other things, relies on the obituary style of c.v. That format fails totally to 'sell' the applicant and, if it lands on the desk of a prospective employer along with fifty similar missives, the chances of it being the one to stand out are nil.

Which means that, once again, readers of this book who adopt its approach are ahead of the field.

To the older job hunter who has become redundant, the question of whether to take a lesser job is often not a matter of choice. Most people in their mid-fifties are well aware of the reduced openings available, and only too pleased to consider almost anything which gets them back into employment – but what are the real handicaps of these extra years in job hunting?

No one will deny that age can be a negative factor, but it can be overstressed. Many older employees are distinctly unhappy in their jobs. Because of their age, they tell themselves that they have no choice but to soldier on, when really they ought to be thinking about the challenge of a new job, new colleagues and a new town, and all the interest which come out of them – it could take ten years off their age! Someone who thinks that the time for moving on has passed has to consider the advantages that age and experience can offer a new employer. With employee numbers being cut back in most companies, those who remain have to justify their keep by offering in-depth experience which youth lacks. Stability, maturity and the ability to remain calm under pressure are all attractive qualities to the discerning employer.

The older job hunters' difficulties lie in bringing their attractions to the notice of people who will value them, and here it has to be pointed out that being 'too old' is relative. In some fields such as advertising, you may be too old at 35. In a 'young' industry, the fact has to be faced that the hirers are going to be thinking in terms of younger applicants, so the initial contact with the firm through a letter of application or c.v. must avoid focusing the reader's mind on chronological history.

Design of c.v.s is discussed later in this chapter, but the older applicant should not hesitate to opt for the functional style, emphasizing problems faced and solutions found, with the obvious message that you can do the same for a new employer. If given the choice, you should apply for posts with a letter rather than any alternative, as this can more easily be written to blur age and years of work experience. Stress should be put on drive and energy, conveying the impression of a vigorous individual who is eager to join a new company and take up new challenges. Age need not be mentioned at this stage, and the letter might only refer to work experience going back a maximum of ten years.

Where completion of an application form is required, it is certain that age will be asked, and there is no escape. *Never* try to 'lose' a few years. Where appropriate, use the opportunity to sell attributes, and try to ensure that the rest of the form looks so interesting that the recipient will not be blinded by the figure in the age box.

Your first objective is to win an interview, and then you must use it to show, in the way which is discussed later in the book, how you could successfully fill the post irrespective of your age, which by then will be known. The need to do well at interview, particularly in the first few minutes, is crucial, and applicants should pay particular attention to appearance. Mutton done up to look like lamb is seldom successful, but try to avoid looking out of condition or sticking to typically middle-aged dress or even spectacle styles – without going too far in the opposite direction. There is no harm in tinting the hair to disguise the encroachment of unwanted grey strands – your friends might take a day or two to get used to the change, but your potential new employers won't know your previous image. If you succeed in meeting them and selling your attributes without having put anyone off by first declaring your age and secondly looking prehistoric, no one has suffered and both you and the new employer have gained.

Age will mean a longer haul for most job hunters who are 'too old', but it is no excuse for giving up – it is a reason to work even harder at self-promotion.

## PERSONAL DATA BANK

Most people realize that they will need to put together a lot of personal information about themselves. It can be very tedious to have to dig this out from many separate places each time an application is made and it pays to bring all your material together at the beginning. Much of the data is obvious – things like date of birth will cause no problems – but some employers even ask for items such as passport numbers and date of validity. Not too many people carry that kind of fact around in their heads! Applicants for public service appointments can expect more probing into their personal backgrounds – often the application form is a lengthy document. The Civil Service Commission, in its wisdom, will even want to know the maiden name of the candidate's mother!

Job hunters should assemble all the basic facts which are likely to be wanted. Each time some application needs a new piece of information, add it to the list, which will grow until it eventually contains everything that there is to know about you. Building a personal data bank also gives you an opportunity to focus on the plus points which you have to offer as well as the minus ones which may need further thought about how best to present them in the least damaging way. Until this exercise is complete, it is dangerous and wrong to try to produce a c.v.

Assembling the data bank is a staged process:

1 Collect facts.
2 After a day or two, review the material and make any alterations that are needed.
3 Decide on your résumé format and layout.
4 Produce the résumé.

Stage 4 will not be reached in ten minutes, and time invested in completing the steps will be time well spent, particularly the writing and rewriting at stage 2 to improve your marketability.

What goes into your data bank? The items suggested in the example given below are the minimum you will need, but ensure that plenty of empty space is left in each section for additions demanded by experience. Building up a data bank in this way is a major task, but a revealing one, and will save time later. More important, it forces you to consider the best way of presenting the wealth of material you will have gathered.

A graduate's personal data bank will clearly not have entries for a number of the categories. As far as possible graduates should make use of their vacation work, if any, to answer questions concerned with previous jobs. Sandwich course students whose experience consists of alternating periods of college and industrial training should refer to their periods of work experience.

## RÉSUMÉ REJECTIONS

If there was a law which prohibited the posting of the many thousands of résumés sent out daily, solicited or otherwise, the Post Office would lose a good deal of income. To look at it from another angle, if a job hunter's résumé is to gain even a few seconds' attention from the recipient, it must be special and stand out. Producing and writing a good résumé is, in times of high unemployment, the most important single stage in job hunting.

## Personal data bank

```
General Information
Name ......................................................
Address...................................................
Telephone: Home...............   Business.........................
Date of birth.................   Age last birthday ..............
Place of birth................   Nationality.....................
Height........................   Weight..........................
Marital status................   Children (no. and ages).........
Passport no.& Expiry date.....   National Insurance No...........
...............................  ................................

Education and training
Schools attended from age 11..........................................
Certificates gained with dates, subjects and grades..............
......................................................................
College/university attended with dates............................
Qualifications/degree awarded with dates..........................
Subjects..............................................................
Languages (state written, spoken, reading standard)..............
......................................................................
Postgraduate courses..................................................
Clubs/societies joined at school and college......................
Offices held..........................................................
Holiday jobs..........................................................
Professional qualifications and dates.............................
......................................................................
Further training courses with dates, length of course and subjects
......................................................................
......................................................................


Military service
Branch of service.............   Rank on discharge...............
Date entered..................   Date left.......................
Service training......................................................

Interests and activities
List clubs, societies, published items, inventions, hobbies, sports,
offices held, etc.....................................................
```

(continues over)

## Building a Résumé

## Personal data bank (continued)

```
Employment
Current/most recent salary..........  Salary objective...........

Immediate job requirements
List five jobs you could fill in order of personal preference
            1..........................
            2..........................
            3..........................
            4..........................
            5..........................

List the two jobs (from the above) for which you are best qualified
            1..........................
            2..........................

State the job title you plan to have in
            1 Five years...............
            2 Ten years................


Current/most recent job
Date joined/date left..............................................
Company............................................................
Business/product...................................................
Annual turnover....................................................
Job title(s).......................................................
Reporting to.......................................................
Number reporting to you............................................
Starting/finishing salary..........................................
Bonuses/allowances etc.............................................
Reason for leaving.................................................
...................................................................
Description of job and responsibilities (note equipment under
your control, proportion of company employees under your
supervision etc.)..................................................
...................................................................
...................................................................
...................................................................
Major accomplishments (refer to savings, costs, sales etc.)........
...................................................................
...................................................................
...................................................................
...................................................................
```

## Personal data bank (continued)

```
List any reports or recommendations which you made and what
happened to them, including technical or administrative
suggestions........................................................
..................................................................
..................................................................
..................................................................

List any major management decisions which you took or recommended
..................................................................
..................................................................
..................................................................

State what promotions you gained with this employer...............
..................................................................
..................................................................
..................................................................

List any other achievement or significant event when with this
employer..........................................................
..................................................................
..................................................................
..................................................................


Previous posts
Repeat the data given above for each of your previous 3 posts.
```

To gain an interview, the chances of success are perhaps one in forty as ten people at maximum will probably be interviewed and there might be around 400 applications for the job. At interview, the chance of being appointed rises to one in ten, assuming there is only one vacancy. These are startling statistics to some people; don't forget them!

The typical résumé sent out by job hunters can only be described as lamentable. It is hard to believe that job hunters expect positive results from some of their efforts. I have seen handwritten résumés from alleged managers which run to five pages in length, while others fill just over half a page. Some actually come on lined paper! Many contain spelling or grammatical errors, and there are always people who think their handwriting should be on a level with that of the most eccentric doctor. If the job hunters who send such résumés were to receive one in a mailbag bringing scores of similar missives, they would condemn it to the waste-bin without further ado. Hirers are busy people and their bins are full of rejected résumés.

## MAKING THE RIGHT IMPRESSION

There is no single kind of résumé which will be right for all job hunters or all hirers, but there are some dos and don'ts. Think about them before deciding on your own preferred format and content.

Some consultants suggest that coloured notepaper – pale grey, perhaps – will stand out in a heap of mail. True, it will, but for every person favourably impressed by this attention-grabber, two or three might be put off. The safest bet is to choose a good quality white notepaper of A4 size with matching envelopes (unless perhaps you are applying to a post where creative flair and an extrovert approach are expected, but it is a possible added risk to be considered carefully).

The résumé *must* be typed, and typed on one side of the paper only – no hirer has the time or inclination to decipher handwriting when there are plenty of clearly typed applications from which to choose. Every town has its secretarial agencies which will type a résumé for a customer at a reasonable price and do it well, but the effect is ruined if the accompanying letter is not produced to the same high standard. Even letters typed in a different typeface will spoil the impression and the solution is either to have everything typed by the same agency or to learn to do the job properly yourself. The latter will take time and effort but independence, in the long run, gives you a flexibility of response which can be important. The skills of clear layout and accurate typing may seem a diversion for the frantic job hunter, and it may be that this is something to be done only by those on whom the pressures are less intense, but they are useful abilities for the future.

Graduates who want to stand out from the crowd must also consider themselves bound by the high standards of presentation recommended for experienced job hunters. Hirers are not under any obligation to give students special dispensation and a faint carbon-copy résumé is just as unimpressive whether it comes from a person of twenty or forty. Students who take the trouble to achieve the quality of presentation recommended in this book will be exceptions, winning benefits in the form of an increased number of interviews.

Some advisers suggest various gimmicks such as producing the résumé in the form of a folded leaflet. Most recipients are conservative by nature, and while ideas like this might be considered by those who are not too concerned about being rejected by anyone who dislikes innovation, the serious job hunter must think hard before departing from the standard presentation.

The document itself can be given various titles but 'Career history' is probably clearest and best.

## Black and white

White space on a sheet of paper is almost as important as anything else. Edge-to-edge typing does not have the same attractions as wall-to-wall carpeting. Unless there is a margin of at least 1 in. at both sides and 1 ¼ to 1 ½ in. at top and bottom, the résumé will look cramped and will discourage the reader.

The best appearance is obtained by using a carbon or black nylon ribbon, which improves the results from even the smallest portable machine. Obviously the result will be even better if you can get access to a good electric typewriter, and the recipient will be keen to read on.

## Layout

Good layout is vital, with the material being balanced and

well organized. If a paragraph happens to end with a word on a line by itself, reword it to avoid an awkward appearance. Subheadings need to be consistently underlined or not; decide on upper or lower case characters. Avoid excessive use of any form of emphasis, such as underlining, as it detracts from the value of such treatment where it is really needed.

### C.V. writers

Organizations exist which, at a price, will prepare curricula vitae for clients and supply copies for distribution. Undoubtedly the finished product looks good, but its reception when coupled with an everyday covering letter is unlikely to be as favourable as you hope and there is a risk that employers will treat it with the same respect or otherwise which they show to the many unwanted mailshots they receive every day.

The content of a c.v., however it is produced, is dependent on the quality of information derived from the personal data bank. Some professional c.v. writers excel in their ability to obtain full information from their clients; others can be superficial. No one can do better in preparing the data than you yourself if you follow the guidance given here and put in the necessary effort.

### Choice of style

The aim of a résumé is to attract favourable interest and lead to an interview. It is the applicant's first and only chance of being considered for the next stage – your personal advertisement, if you like. Choosing the best way to present yourself is your big decision; style is important, and your decision will depend on the job you seek – the more traditional employers will be more likely to respond to traditional presentation.

There are three basic styles, all with many variations:

1. *Obituary*. This has already been briefly mentioned and consists of a list of schools and colleges attended, dates, qualifications gained, company names, job titles and duties.
2. *Historical*. This is a style which gives education information and job details going back, in the latter case, no more than ten years. Earlier experience is treated in a summarized form. The government agency PER recommends this presentation and, well produced, it is good for careers which show unbroken progress. Students will also find this style appropriate – see chapter 9.
3. *Functional*. A functional résumé groups experience by functions such as production, personnel, supervision and so on. It is particularly useful where there have been many job changes which might give the impression of a job hopper, but is not suitable for students who have no work experience.

Examples of the way in which one person's data can be presented in each of the three main styles are given below.

## THE RÉSUMÉ THAT SELLS

Résumés are introductions. They are intended to make the potential employer want to see the applicant and, if this is achieved, the résumé will be read again after the interview. A number of people might see your résumé and so it has to keep selling your attributes, but it must not do so too blatantly.

The material must be well written and stress achievements rather than merely list duties. Employers want to know what you could do for them, not what your routine duties were over the past decade. State your achievements in terms of increased sales, profits or cost savings and use exciting or lively sounding words. The words you use can add to or detract from the verifiable facts of your qualifications. Phrases

## Building a Résumé

## Examples of résumé styles: 1   Obituary

```
                    C A R E E R   H I S T O R Y

NAME              John William SMITH

ADDRESS           25 Oak Crescent, Anyville, Newtown, Midshire
                  Telephone: Newtown (0987) 65432

AGE               36 years

MARITAL STATUS    Married with two children, ages 12 and 10 years

EDUCATION         1956-63 Smallville Primary School, Smallville
                  1963-64 Oldtown Grammar School, Oldtown
                  1964-69 Newway Comprehensive School, Spilltown

QUALIFICATIONS    A level Eng.Lit.(grade B), Eng.Lang.(C),
                  Maths(C), Physics(C)
                  B.Sc.(Class II) Eng., Greybrick University 1973
                  Member of Institute of Hydraulic Engineers, 1980
                  Member of Institute of Technical Managers, 1983

EXPERIENCE        September 1973 - March 1976
                  Flash Designs Ltd, Irontown
                  Draughtsman in design office

                  April 1976 - June 1978
                  Brightmetal Creations Ltd, Countrytown
                  Senior designer

                  July 1978 - February 1979
                  Pinchpenny Company Ltd, Westown
                  Technical manager, responsible for 4 staff

                  February 1979 - May 1979
                  Redundant on closure of above company

                  June 1979 - October 1983
                  Plodding Manufacturing Ltd, Canalville
                  Production controller then production manager
                  responsible for 40 staff

                  November 1983 - Present day
                  Phoenix Engineering Ltd, Newtown
                  Engineering manager responsible for 22 staff

INTERESTS         Photography and model engineering
```

should be very carefully constructed to convey strength and honesty. Use brief and direct sentences and avoid complex subclauses. An open, natural tone is better than impersonal, third-person language. Words like 'established', 'planned', 'managed' will make more impact than long phrases which say the same thing but lose the meaning in a torrent of words. Pompous or long-winded expressions are best avoided: for example, 'at that moment in time' should be replaced by

## 2 Historical

```
                    C A R E E R  H I S T O R Y

NAME            John William SMITH

ADDRESS         25 Oak Crescent, Anyville, Newtown, Midshire
                Telephone: Newtown (0987) 65432

BORN            September 9  1951

FAMILY          Married with two children, ages 12 and 10 years

EDUCATION       1956-63 Smallville Primary School, Smallville
                1963-64 Oldtown Grammar School, Oldtown
                1964-69 Newway Comprehensive School, Spilltown
                1969-73 Greybrick University.  B.Sc.(II), Eng.

PROFESSIONAL    Member of Institute of Hydraulic Engineers, 1980
                Member of Institute of Technical Managers, 1983

WORK EXPERIENCE
1978-79         Technical Manager with Pinchpenny Company. With
                this company, I was responsible for a department
                of four people engaged in designing machines
                for industry to be produced at the lowest
                possible capital cost to the purchaser without
                loss of reliability. A fall in the demand
                for new equipment caused the company to close.

1979-83         First appointed as Production Controller with
                the Plodding Manufacturing company. Then, within
                15 months, I became Production Manager with
                a staff of 40 engaged in manufacturing components
                for the makers of a range of domestic appliances.

1983-now        As Engineering Manager with the Phoenix Engineer-
                ing company, I head the design and quality
                control departments with a staff of over 20
                people. The machinery built by the company
                is purchased by firms manufacturing consumer
                durables at home and overseas.

1973-78         My earlier experience was in design engineering
                with two companies which were involved in
                supplying equipment to manufacturing industry.

LEISURE         Member of local camera club
                Committee member of model engineering club
                Occasional squash player
```

'then'; 'as a result of' should become 'because', and so on. There are many other phrases of this type; ban them all and replace them by the simpler alternatives.

Most people have some words which they cannot spell without some head-scratching no matter how good they usually are at spelling. The number of times I have seen 'liason', 'committment' and 'developement' gives cause for concern. Anyone can have a spelling lapse, but what kind of

# 3 Functional

## CAREER HISTORY

John William SMITH, 25 Oak Crescent, Anyville, Newtown, Midshire
Tel: Newtown (0987) 65432

**OBJECTIVE**

An engineering management appointment with career opportunity and challenge. I am qualified to contribute to the management team and the engineering technology at senior level in an organization.

**GENERAL BACKGROUND**

Experienced manager with 14 years' proven achievement in design and management in companies manufacturing medium sized equipment for industrial and domestic use.

I have worked in various parts of the UK and am willing to relocate. Aged 36, married and with two children (ages 12 and 10), I am in excellent health. A graduate of Greybrick University (B.Sc.,Eng.), I am a Member of the Institute of Hydraulic Engineers and the Institute of Technical Managers.

My personal strengths include an ability to motivate staff and I enjoy being part of a management team as well as working on individual projects.

I have had two items published in my Institute journal on technical developments which I have pioneered.

### AREAS OF MAJOR EXPERIENCE

**DESIGN**

In 6 years, I progressed from basic design work in Flash Designs (makers of industrial machinery) to Technical Manager with Pinchpenny where I controlled a staff of 4. In that post, I reduced the manufacturing costs by 12% of previous levels in under one year while improving product reliability.

**PRODUCTION**

With the Plodding Manufacturing company, I increased the machine utilization by a third and reduced the cost of production by over 15% as Production Controller and then Production Manager over a 4 year period. I was responsible for approximately 40 staff. Turnover, in real terms, increased by more than 20% during my employment with this firm.

**TECHNICAL & QUALITY**

Currently, I control the quality function at Phoenix Engineering through a staff of 10 and I also manage a 12 strong design team which develops machinery for use by manufacturers of consumer durables. Quality complaints have fallen by 75% since I established new control systems and our production costs have been reduced by over 25% through design changes alone without loss of reliability.

candidates, aware of the dangers, would not double-check every word in their résumés? The employer is bound to think that spelling errors are indicative of sloppy work in other spheres – and so another résumé bites the dust.

## IMPORTANCE OF PRESENTATION

The importance of the way in which the résumé presents the individual cannot be overstated. Your competitors will often be as well if not better qualified than you, but with poorer and duller presentation they will not be able to do themselves justice. They will, of course, be proud of their efforts, but will lose out by being ordinary. Some may even unwittingly give away facts which will prompt immediate rejection, for at this stage no one knows exactly what the employer is seeking.

That is why an achievement-orientated résumé is usually best as it catches the recipient's interest and plays down your weaknesses. Key information must be offered in such a way that hirers can make a quick, positive decision to interview you. This achieved, the first hurdle has been successfully cleared – which was the object of the exercise.

## USING YOUR RÉSUMÉ

Having read so much about the preparation and production of an outstanding résumé, the reader must now prepare for a shock – standard résumés should *not* be sent out in response to a specific advertisement even when a résumé is requested, and certainly not to any particular company to which you may have written speculatively. Consider the thoughts of employers.

They have particular vacancies to fill and will be deluged with résumés giving general information about the applicants. Some of that material will be irrelevant to those particular jobs, some will be too sparse, and hirers will be left trying to pick out the bits they want and wondering if they contain the germ of what the candidates could do for them.

Picking up the successful job hunter's résumé, specially written for each post, employers will respond much more favourably to this person whose experience more closely fits their needs. The message is clear. Using your chosen style and personal data bank, write out a résumé angled to suit the job advertised or the company to which you are writing speculatively, keeping to the approach you have used in the general résumé. Augment the sections most relevant to the job and reduce the other parts. Your positive response rate will increase measurably – assuming, of course, that your experience meets the needs of the job in the first place!

It is best to keep your general résumé for sending to recruitment agencies, where it will be considered against the wide range of vacancies they handle for a multitude of companies. Of course, this restricted use of general résumés means more work for you, but it will be more fruitful work which will help you concentrate on applying only for those jobs where there is a fair match of skills and needs. It also adds to the argument in favour of typing your own material independently as no c.v. writing company will entertain the notion of a separate résumé for every application.

# 3
# Locating Employers and Jobs

Having produced a fully stocked personal data bank and an excellent résumé for general use with recruitment agencies or, in modified form, for answering advertisements, your next stage is to find potential employers and jobs. There are numerous sources and the major ones are reviewed below. In each case, it is important to approach your source in a way which makes you stand out from the competition.

**PERSONAL CONTACTS**

Many jobs are filled this way and some people refer to it, disparagingly, as the 'Grapevine'. This implied criticism should not deter you, and the higher up the ladder you are, the more important this approach can become. Remember the employers' viewpoint. If they have vacancies to fill, they have a degree of risk ahead of them and if they hear of someone – you – who has the skills they seek and who is recommended by a friend of a friend, their confidence increases. You get the chance to convince them that you are the right choice for the job. If you can't meet employers' needs, you don't get the job, but you have lost nothing by having been recommended and have added to your interview experience and knowledge of companies in your field.

Your contacts might include former employers, business contacts, suppliers, your bank manager, professional institute colleagues, social club contacts (such as Round Table or Lions), solicitors, local authority friends, MPs, councillors, friends, neighbours, relatives and many more. Most people will be able to add significantly to that list, but it provides a basis – a useful number of potential leads which may throw up possible jobs or pointers to others who can help.

At the same time, the introductions which come through these channels can be misleading because friends and acquaintances, anxious to help, will suggest unsuitable possibilities. Don't ignore them, as they can lead to more useful contacts and firms. The message about personal contacts must inevitably be that you should use them but not be carried away with high hopes which, quite often, will come to nothing.

## SOCIAL AND PUBLIC ORGANIZATIONS

Anyone seeking a new job needs to cultivate contacts with influential people who might be of assistance. Obviously, this is best done before your need becomes urgent, but it is never too late to begin. Active involvement in your trade association or union, Chamber of Commerce, professional institute and the like will bring you into close touch with people who carry authority at the various meetings, seminars, dinners and official events. If the choice lies between an evening spent sitting in front of the television or attending a boring dinner, then there is no question that the right thing to do is to dust off the best clothes and learn to mingle.

Increased exposure to people who count can come in other ways; one method of keeping your name in front of the 'right' people is to write for your trade press. Professional journals are always glad to hear from occasional contributors and, as well as earning you a few pounds, your article will ensure that your name and perhaps even your picture are seen in relevant circles all over the country.

If you are already a leading light in your own favourite organization, this might be the time to extend into other societies or to think about planning some event which just happens to give you a bit of personal publicity at the same time. Adding to your involvement in local affairs can only help you; the more active you are, the wider will be your exposure.

Political associations can open many doors, but bear in mind that the opposing party is unlikely to accept your sudden conversion to its cause! Political interest should never be mentioned in contact with an employer – it may be sufficient to rule you out immediately if you are of the 'wrong' persuasion. Exceptions would be cases where the job is related to politics or you know the employer's views – but tread carefully in the latter case to avoid any hint of trying to gain favour by flattery.

## TRADE SHOWS

Trade shows are not to be ignored if you want to remain in your present industry as they bring together under one roof a large number of people from all levels. You must be prepared to wait long hours in the hope that sooner or later the senior people from major firms will be walking around. Even if you only manage to talk to a relatively junior person on a stand, you can find out when the top brass are expected to visit. Try to find out about developments within the company so that, when the decision-makers arrive, you can talk with apparent knowledge of plans for the firm or its products. If you learn that the senior staff are not visiting on the days you are there, you can at least find out their names; in future, when you write or telephone, you will know to whom you want to talk.

Even if you cannot attend the show for some reason, you

might consider obtaining a copy of the programme, which will list the exhibitors and perhaps even some of the people attending. That opens up the possibility of your doing a round of the hotels where these people might be staying, when you can make contact in the bars and lobbies. The informality of such meetings can make it easy to talk and any invitation to follow up your encounter can open new doors.

## CUES FROM THE NEWS

The trade, national and local press regularly publish news about organizations and their new products, take-overs, closures, industrial problems, expansion plans and so on. These can suggest useful openings to pursue. Full addresses and telephones numbers are easily found in directories available in public libraries; you can then write to the appropriate person saying that you have noticed a particular news item. Taking your cue from the nature of the report, you may be able to point out how your experience could be useful to the firm in its development of a new product or expansion programme. A sample of a speculative letter is given below. If you receive no answer to a letter, there is nothing to lose by a second contact – you can only be told 'No'.

There are distinct advantages to this approach. You will probably be the only person to have written and your letter will demonstrate initiative at a time when the company may really need help. If your letter reaches the kind of person who responds positively, there are all the signs of a good match between someone (you) who seizes an opening when it appears and a boss who encourages such an individual. It could be the beginning of a long-running show!

The value of personal contacts depends to a great extent on your willingness to try every usual and unusual possibility which crosses your mind. There are, without doubt, hundreds of opportunities for enterprising people to explore; the only limit is your own imagination.

## Sample speculative letter to a company

```
                            25 Oak Crescent,
                            Anyville,
                            Newtown,
                            Midshire.

                            14 March 1988

Mr J E Brown,
Managing Director,
Futuristic Equipment PLC,
Northern Industrial Estate,
Brightown-on-Sea,
Coastshire.

Dear Mr Brown,

Your company's latest development in the design of machinery
to manufacture disposable garden furniture was examined in
this month's edition of Manufacturing Services. I found the
article most thought-provoking and agree with the philosophy
behind your plans.

As a manager with over 15 years' professional experience, I
believe that my background may be of interest to you.

For the past 5 years, I have been Engineering Manager with
a company employing over 100 people, and I am responsible for
the design and quality control functions. I have direct respon-
sibility for 22 staff.

In this post, my achievements have included:

        initiating quality control studies which have reduced
        quality problems by 75%,

        leading a team of designers who have reduced costs
        by 25%,

        advising customers on design changes which have
        saved one major firm over 20% in its production costs.

Aged 36, I am married with two children. I have a B.Sc.(Eng.)
degree and am a Member of the Institute of Hydraulic Engineers
and the Institute of Technical Managers.

I am confident that a meeting with you would be of mutual benefit
and would allow me to explain the relevance of my experience
to the challenges which the article foresees for your company.

Within the next few days, I will telephone your office and
hope to arrange a meeting with you.

Yours sincerely,


John W Smith
```

## ADVERTISED VACANCIES

Approximately 60 per cent of jobs are filled through advertisements, so it is easy to understand why job hunters turn to the press for an answer to their needs. The *Daily Telegraph* and the *Sunday Times* are the major national newspapers specializing in a full range of 'Situations Vacant', but specialist posts appear in other newspapers and those looking for finance jobs will not need to be reminded that the *Financial Times* is the paper for their field. Regional and specialist trade newspapers should not be overlooked; they have the advantage of a lower circulation, making competition less intense for applicants.

Since so many people respond to advertisements, it is even more important that job hunters put forward a powerful case for interview which will stand out above the others, bringing the desired invitation to meet the company representative and discuss matters further. Despite the competition, you will find that use of the methods and materials recommended in this book will bring you an increased number of openings – a point which you can check by comparing the results before and after you employ this approach.

When you see an advertisement which looks interesting, read it briefly. Read it a second time and underline the main requirements of the job, relating them to your own abilities and experience. Ask yourself 'Do I want the job?', and then 'Can I do it?' If the answers are 'Yes', then apply. Cut out and keep the advertisement, writing on it the publication and date.

Advertisers seldom find candidates who completely meet their needs as stated, so it can be worth applying even if you do not quite match the specification. Clearly, if the advertisement makes a big point of age and stipulates that 35 is the top limit, it is not worth the postage stamp to apply if you are 50. But if the problem is that you do not possess exactly the right degree though you have comparable qualifications plus relevant experience, it is time to start thinking about how you are going to win your invitation to an interview. There may be vacancies for someone of greater seniority: here you might be successful if you nearly match up and can be hired at a lower salary. Again, the applicant eventually chosen may need new staff and you could be in line for a job once he or she has settled in. You might even discover where the successful candidate came from and fill the post now left vacant!

Having identified a suitable advertisement, your next step is to telephone the company, asking to speak to whoever is doing the hiring 'to obtain further details of the post'. Have a list of points you want to raise ready prepared before telephoning and then discuss the job with the decision-maker. *Never* indicate by the merest suggestion any point on which you fall short and could be rejected. To say that you notice the requirement is for someone with ten years' experience but would they consider you even although you have only six is giving the company an obvious opportunity to reject you before you have had a chance to show your value in other ways. Ask for an application form and copy of the job description before ending the conversation with a 'Thank you for your help'.

You are, by now, one step ahead of the competition – your name and voice are known to the company; you have declared your interest and shown some initiative. Don't be put off if your effort at telephone contact does not succeed. You may have surprised the employer and perhaps caught him or her off guard, but you have certainly lost nothing and may have gained a lot.

Write to the advertiser saying 'Further to our conversation on —, I confirm that I can match the requirements for the position of —', and then show how you do so. If there is an application form, return it with a covering letter drawing attention to those attributes which are particularly important in the post. If there is no application form and you are invited to send a résumé, angle it towards the particular job as explained in chapter 2. Another alternative is that you may be invited to write a letter of application, and here you should follow the general principles of selling your skills and pointing to what you can do for the advertiser. A sample covering letter to accompany a résumé (or, with minor modification, an application form) and a sample letter of application are given below. Not every company is particularly well organ-

## Sample letter to company or agency in reply to an advertisement

> 25 Oak Crescent,
> Anyville,
> Newtown,
> Midshire.
>
> 14 March 1988
>
> Mr R T Green,
> Managing Director,
> Bigtime Engineering PLC,
> Grease Street,
> Blackchester.
>
> Dear Mr Green,
>
> Your Company's advertisement for an Engineering and Technical Manager interests me considerably and my qualifications match those required for the appointment.
>
> For the past 15 years, I have held positions of increasing responsibility in engineering design work. I currently control the quality and technical departments in a leading company which manufactures machinery for the consumer durable industry. This involves direct responsiblity for 22 staff.
>
> In this post, my achievements have included:
>
> > initiating quality control studies which have reduced quality problems by 75%,
> >
> > leading a team of designers who have reduced costs by 25%,
> >
> > advising customers on design changes which have saved one major firm over 20% in its production costs.
>
> My earlier experience included 4 years in production management, where I reduced costs by 15% and raised productivity. As Technical Manager in another company, I improved reliability of the products and saved 12% on manufacturing costs in one year.
>
> Aged 36, I am married and have two children. I hold a B.Sc.(Eng.) degree and am a Member of the Institute of Hydraulic Engineers and the Institute of Technical Managers. I am in excellent health and would have no problems in moving to Blackchester.
>
> I am keen to find a new challenge where my experience can be applied and my career furthered. Your company is offering such an opportunity and my background meets your requirements.
>
> I look forward to hearing from you and to receiving a copy of the job description, if available.
>
> Yours sincerely,
>
> John W Smith

**NB**: change 'company' to 'client' when writing to a recruitment agency.

ized and careful with incoming mail and wise job hunters will staple together all material which they send – curricula vitae, application forms and covering letters.

Following an application, if you have received no response after two weeks, telephone and reaffirm your interest in the job you have discussed on the telephone and since confirmed in writing, giving the dates of both contacts. Tell the

**Cover letter for a c.v. in reply to an advertisement**

```
                                        25 Oak Crescent,
                                        Anyville,
                                        Newtown,
                                        Midshire.
   Mr R T Green,                        14 March 1988
   Managing Director,
   Bigtime Engineering PLC,
   Grease Street,
   Blackchester.

   Dear Mr Green,
   Your company's advertisement for an Engineering and Technical
   Manager interests me considerably and my qualifications match
   those required for the appointment.
   For the past 15 years, I have held positions of increasing
   responsibility in engineering design work. At present I
   control the quality and technical departments in a leading
   company which manufactures machinery for the consumer durable
   industry, and am responsible for 22 people.
   In the past year, my achievements have included:

        Initiating quality control studies to improve further
        the reliability of our designs; this has resulted in an
        annual saving of £25,000 in one machine alone.

        Working with customers, I have reviewed their planned
        component designs and savings of over 20% have been
        recorded by a major domestic appliance manufacturer for
        tooling costs.

   Throughout my career, I have been able to reduce costs and
   improve productivity wherever I have worked. I now seek an
   opportunity to contribute in a larger organization.
   I am enclosing my career history which gives an outline of
   my experience. I would welcome an opportunity of discussing
   the appointment with you when I could give further details
   of my background and how it relates to your company.
   I look forward to hearing further from you and receiving a
   copy of the job description, if one is available.

   Yours sincerely,

   John W Smith
```

**NB: change 'company' to 'client' when writing to a recruitment agency.**

company that you realize that mail can go astray, ask if your letter has been received and enquire what is happening to your application.

Advertisements appear in many publications and it is impossible for the job hunter to buy them all. Many are available in public libraries; visit yours at least twice every week. Librarians will invariably be pleased to tell you what journals they take and, in some cases, will even obtain a special one for you if it is not already on their list. Recent economies have caused a cutback on many shelves but a serious request will always be treated helpfully.

## PER

Professional and Executive Recruitment (PER) is the government's own recruitment agency for all qualified individuals, which means those with A levels and above. To contact PER, ask at your local Jobcentre; enrolment is free.

PER has changed its method of operation many times over the years but currently those on its register receive a free weekly copy of *Executive Post* sent to their homes, and it is up to job hunters to apply for jobs advertised in it. The number of appointments advertised is usually well in excess of 300 but there is no obligation for a company to notify PER of its vacancies, so do not expect the paper to cover every possible opportunity.

*Executive Post* also gives guidance on possibilities such as franchising, institute membership and the preparation of a c.v. It is all useful advice worth taking into consideration but, because it is so freely available, any applicants who, for example, stick rigidly to the suggestions on laying out a c.v. will find themselves part of a very large crowd of people presenting themselves in an identical way. Even when you apply to PER advertisements, you will gain by being different and using the methods explained here. Think of the relief to the advertiser who picks up a résumé which does not follow the same lines as the previous 372! The writer of this breath of fresh air must be well on the way to an interview by the time his or her first paragraph has been read.

Various training courses are also run by PER, and job hunters may find one or more of these useful. They vary from half-day seminars to courses lasting several weeks at a college or university. Eligibility conditions may vary, so it is important to check if you intend to apply.

PER services, but not all of its courses, are open to those who are employed as well as those who are unemployed.

## AGENCIES, CONSULTANCIES AND REGISTERS

There are many reputable agencies and consultancies which handle vacancies for companies. In some cases they send replies direct to the firm; in others they screen the applicants before producing a shortlist for the company to see. It is best to treat advertisements by third parties as if the advertiser was the actual hirer. Telephone calls to agencies can sometimes be disappointing – the consultant may know very little about the post – but on other occasions, this approach can be very informative. A preliminary talk to a consultant is always worth trying and, as in direct approaches to companies, it can create a good impression at an early stage in the application.

Lists of the names and addresses of consultants are easily available from many sources; the most complete will be found in the *Personnel and Training Yearbook* available in most libraries. This publication gives the names of the directors of the organization and the area in which they specialize. A model covering letter for sending with a c.v. to recruitment agencies is shown below.

As well as answering agency advertisements, you might choose to contact them independently. If you do, it is important to be selective: some agencies operate only in a specific industry, some cover functions found in all industries, such

## 42 Locating Employers and Jobs

**Sample cover letter for a speculative c.v. to a recruitment agency**

```
                                    25 Oak Crescent,
                                    Anyville,
                                    Newtown,
                                    Midshire.

                                    14 March 1988

Mrs C L Black,
Managing Director,
Findem Recruitment Agency,
Poshtowers,
High Street,
Washborough.


Dear Mrs Black,

As part of your service to client companies, you may have an
assignment which requires an experienced Engineering or
Technical Manager.

My background includes responsible appointments with two highly
respected companies, Phoenix Engineering (my current employer)
and the Plodding Manufacturing Company. I have held these posts
for a total of nine years.

Throughout my career I have worked in design and production
of engineering components or industrial machinery, and I have
a record of raising quality standards and cutting costs on
a wide range of products.

The enclosed résumé briefly outlines my achievements over my
15 years of industrial experience. I am currently seeking an
appointment as Engineering Manager in a company where my qualifi-
cations could be used and where I would find new challenges.

If I meet the requirements of one of your clients, I would
very much welcome the chance of discussing my background further
with you.

I look forward to hearing from you.

Yours sincerely,



John W Smith
```

as accountancy, and others are general, covering a range of industries and disciplines. A few will only take on assignments above a certain salary level.

If the job hunter's background does not suit any posts which the agency is handling at that moment, the chance of the applicant's being remembered in a few months' time when an appropriate assignment comes along is not good unless the agency has a good retrieval system – which not all have. It makes sense to select your agencies carefully and then contact them at intervals to remind them of your interest and qualifications.

Agents can earn their fees from the client company or the job hunter. In the former case, always remember that the agent's duty is to serve the client company, whose interest will come first. Firms which charge the job hunter offer varying consultancy services; individual career counselling, design of curricula vitae, even marketing you in every respect. These agencies should be searching their lists to find you a niche but you must be clear from the outset exactly what you will get for your money and how long the service will work for you.

Anyone choosing this course of action is unlikely to need the detailed advice offered in this book – you will receive full guidance as part of your counselling. The only thing to add is that you should take the greatest possible care to ensure that you use only firms with impeccable reputations, as many new and unproven organizations have set up shop in these difficult times which have very little to offer their clients. Cheap services can prove extortionate in the long run for the value they provide.

## BOX NUMBERS

Unless you want to swell Post Office profits, forget them. Your chance of getting a reply is remote and there is a possibility you might reveal your desire to move to the wrong person – even your own employer! On the positive side, because most people will not respond to a box number, the competition is reduced, but it is still not a good bet. Too often, box numbers are merely a way for advertisers to escape their obligations to reply to applicants; any reputable firm can find better ways of finding staff without revealing their name, if that is their policy.

## TIMING IT RIGHT

When you reply to an advertised vacancy, timing can be important. If you can get your letter in on the first day after the advertisement appears, yours will be one of only 2 per cent of the total number of applications. The second day will see the arrival of about 20 per cent of the responses and the third day will bring about 40 per cent. The numbers will begin to fall off after this and by the end of the week about 90 per cent of the replies will have been received, with a mere trickle thereafter. It is not to your advantage to have your carefully prepared application lost in the crowd, and unless you can guarantee delivery on the first day, it is best to wait until the peak has passed. No company is going to fill the job in the first day or two and you have nothing to lose and something to gain by holding your fire. But don't delay too long – it might suggest only casual interest in the post.

## DIRECT APPROACH

The advantage of the direct approach which stands out above all else is that the applicant can present an enterprising image and will almost certainly be the sole applicant. If you decide to try this method, you must write to the decision-maker by name, something which can be discovered by a simple telephone call and a word with the firm's switchboard operator.

   The direct approach can tap openings which have yet to appear, but, if it is to be successful, the letter needs to arrive on the right desk at the right time. When companies are seeking to contain or reduce costs, they will be looking at their salary bill and looking twice at the possibility of cutting out all but essential staff. The chance of the arrival of your letter being welcome is remote and the job hunter who uses this method of finding work must face the prospect of a very low response rate when things are tight in the business world. Senior managers are fully aware of the high cost of recruitment and if outstanding people present their talents, jobs can appear overnight. People do get jobs in this way and anyone can strike lucky, but it is a method requiring the greatest patience.

When writing speculative letters to companies (see the sample above, page 33), *never* include a résumé. A personal letter is the only approach likely to succeed and this should emphasize your past achievements and indicate what you could do for your next employer. The letter should concentrate on the company and how you can help it. It must not begin with a sentence which says that you are looking for a job, or this will be the first and last sentence that is read.

Telephone calls are not recommended as the first step in a direct approach. They are unlikely to reach the right person and even if they do get through, they allow no time for consideration. In these circumstances, the likely answer is 'No', and an opportunity is lost. If you do decide on the direct written approach, though, there are ways in which the positive response rate can be increased:

Writing to the individual by name is essential.
An individually written letter aimed at a particular company stands a better chance of a reply than a circular-type letter or letter plus résumé.

Limit your letter to one side of A4 paper. Each additional paragraph means less chance of the letter's being read.

Stick to good quality white paper and matching envelopes.

Mark the envelope 'Personal', which improves its chance of reaching its target.

Keep the sentences short, clear and simple. Paragraphs should not exceed six lines.

Sign the letter with a blue ballpoint or fountain pen. The broad line produced by a nylon-tip pen may suggest that you are trying to impose your authority, and recipients are unlikely to hire anyone who might be stronger than they are.

Sign the letter with your full first name, initials and surname, not just initials and surname.

Show that you have industry knowledge in your letter.

Concentrate on career plans, not just job possibilities.

Make no reference to money.

Write your letter in a bright and enthusiastic tone.

Read the draft letter aloud to find the correct words; avoid phrases which are cold or complicated.

Don't waste your time sending out speculative letters at holiday times – concentrate on spring and autumn.

Post your letter so that it does not arrive on a Monday or Friday, days when people are often absent from the office or too preoccupied with their weekend activities.

Never offer any reason why you are looking for a job – it does nothing for whoever reads your story, as they are only interested in what you might do for their company.

Remember that postage and your time are expensive; do not waste your efforts on the wrong companies. Libraries have many directories, so make sure that you only write to companies in your field.

All the skills you need to answer an advertisement or prepare a good résumé are even more essential if the direct approach is to pay off. Quality materials, properly targeted and personally addressed, coupled with succinct content, are fundamental – anything else is a waste of time.

Graduates trying a direct approach must be prepared for a long haul. Thoughtful job hunting methods will make the applicant stand out against the more usual student approach.

Don't be tempted to cut corners: the real need is to concentrate on quality, achieving the highest possible standards and thereby raising your success rate. It is more productive to spend time and effort in pursuing one well-researched contact than making five or six half-hearted attempts which will get nowhere.

## HEAD-HUNTERS

This is the name given to consultants who are retained to fill the most senior posts in organizations. They set about their work by drawing up a list of the most suitable individuals for the specified job. It is unlikely that you would know in the early stages that your name appears on the list. The vacancy may not be public knowledge and the first that you or any candidate will know will be when you receive a discreet enquiry from the consultant to ascertain your interst. If you are on this select circuit, you have no worries about job hunting – the head-hunters are hunting you!

## 'SITUATIONS WANTED' ADVERTISEMENTS

Putting a 'Situation Wanted' advertisement in a newspaper is a thought which often occurs to an anxious job hunter. Beware: this is likely to be a completely fruitless task. The chance of a decision-maker reading your three or four lines is virtually nil and most replies – if you get any – will be from recruitment agencies offering to put you on their books at some fee or from c.v. writers promoting their services. Any companies that do respond will be small and unlikely to meet anything more than the most modest salary expectations.

Self-advertising in trade or institute journals can be more effective and costs are lower than in national newspapers, so that a semi-display advertisement can be placed for a reasonable price. Advice on presentation and layout will probably be available from the Advertisement Manager of your local newspaper; use this experience if you can. If you decide to persevere with such a method, you may need to take steps to prevent your present employer finding out; a box number or, better, the name and address of a friend from outside the trade could be the answer.

Self-advertising on local radio and television has had spectacular results for the few who have tried it. The novelty of this approach has caught the public's attention and press publicity but, like most things, if it became usual, it would be unlikely to have lasting value as a source of jobs. Gimmicks can bring results if they are new to an area; if this tactic has not been tried in your district, it could be worth investigating.

# 4
# Dealing with Application Forms and Tests

From the point of view of employers, application forms have many advantages. They collect information in a consistent format, allowing easy comparison of candidates and ensuring that important questions are asked and answered. Seen from the job hunter's position, application forms are among the most dangerous inventions since gunpowder. They take a considerable time to complete and always seem to ask the questions you least want to answer. They cause great frustration by giving you little opportunity to sell your achievements while losing no chance to pinpoint your individual weaknesses.

Unfortunately, there is no escape from completing an application form if you hope to be invited for an interview with a firm which uses this system. There are, however, ways in which you can make the best of a bad job.

As with other applications, a typed response is recommended so, if possible, type in your answers to the various questions. Remember that the spaces provided will not be designed to suit you and it may be difficult to fit everything in; check through the form very carefully before beginning. One way to ensure a neat appearance is to photocopy the form and use the copy for practice. If typing is impossible and you are forced to complete the form in your own hand, print the information as neatly as possible. Take your time –

errors are harder to conceal when handwritten. Avoid being pushed into a situation where you are asked to complete a form at the interview – you need to take the form home and complete it carefully to do yourself justice.

When asked to give your employment history, make sure you make the best use of the space to amplify your achievements. If that means you have to summarize the earlier jobs you have held, too bad. You want to promote your strengths, not just provide the equivalent of an obituary style c.v. Ignore questions about past salaries: anything earned five or more years ago is irrelevant and your current salary is for you to keep confidential until you choose to disclose it. If you are asked to state the salary you want, either ignore the question completely or quote a bandwidth of around 20 per cent, encompassing the anticipated rate for the job. If you think the likely salary will be around £18,000, then the range £18,000 to £22,000 would be appropriate.

If you are asked for school and college subjects and examination results, avoid giving grades unless they are really good. If you didn't do too well, you won't want to reduce your chances by admitting it, especially if your formal education ended twenty or more years ago. After a few years' job experience, it matters little what academic standards you achieved, and it is always a source of amazement that companies persist in asking about them when there are so many more relevant things to discover about applicants.

Make sure that any referees you nominate are informed immediately of your use of their names. You should ask them in advance, but even then warn them that they may be telephoned.

If you are asked to state your leisure activities, offer a broad range from active interests to social or local affairs. Never admit to political involvement as your future employer may be a rabid supporter of another party! (Obviously with some jobs, for example in journalism or politically-related posts, this may not apply.)

Do not be tempted to write flowery phrases in any space

which invites you to state additional points in support of your application. Use it to build up your achievements, giving information similar to the type shown in the functional style career history on page 26 under the heading 'Areas of major experience'.

If asked why you left a previous job, never indicate a row with the boss. Whoever was to blame, it looks as if you do not get along with people and that will not help your candidature. The safest answer to give is 'career advancement' or 'promotion' – if you are asked at interview to enlarge upon this, it should be possible for you to show that your career did benefit from the move even if you know it can only be said with hindsight!

When applying to conventional firms or institutions, female applicants should think hard about using 'Ms' if a title is asked – it is not yet a form of address which is accepted universally and can invite disapproval in some quarters. Usage of Ms is increasing but it is not yet universally accepted and job hunters should tread carefully, partically in fields which tend to be conservative.

Never return an application form without a well-written covering letter. Minor adaptation of the sample letter to accompany a career history (see page 37) will provide a suitable example. Finally, return the application form to the employer in an envelope which allows you to fold the form as it was folded when sent to you – a much-folded form does not look good and is to be avoided. The cover letter should be securely stapled to the document to prevent loss – paper clips are too easily dislodged.

All application forms should be copied before you return them – you want to be able to refresh your memory on how you presented yourself before you go for interview. This is particularly important for Civil Service appointments where the standard application form asks candidates for details of previous applications to the Service. Clearly, the earlier application might be referred to by the interviewers so you must not appear to have given inconsistent information. There is no need to repeat the previous details exactly and there can be no criticism for changing the emphasis of your presentation to suit the particular post.

The answers should be angled to suit the information available to you through the advertisement and, if in any doubt, draft out your replies before writing them on the form. If a question does not apply to you, write in the words 'not applicable'. To leave a blank suggests you overlooked the item; to use an abbreviation may be meaningful to you but not the recipient. A dash will be required where a salary figure is requested.

The greatest annoyance of all is the company which invites you to send full personal details in response to an advertisement and, in return, asks you to complete its application form. It is tempting to ignore the request as it tells you something about the firm and its organization, or lack of it, but if you want the job badly enough, you can only grin and bear it. But be warned by what this suggests about the set-up with which you are dealing.

## HANDWRITING TESTS

Some employers particularly ask for application forms to be completed in the candidate's own hand. Generally this is to check on neatness of presentation, but occasionally your application will be submitted to a graphologist who will interpret and report on your personality. There is much disagreement on the validity of this practice but some points are probably fairly made.

> Irregular spacing between words might indicate untidiness and lack of organization.
>
> Excessive flourishes with large, aggressive letters may be the hallmark of a show-off.
>
> Writing over a word or letter twice is said to suggest dishonesty.

Writing which slopes to the left (by a right-handed person) is thought to be a sign of someone lacking in human feeling.

A rounded style of writing is sometimes the sign of an immature person.

However accurate or otherwise these observations may be, the fact is that some firms believe in them and they can affect your application for a post. The safest way to deal with handwriting requests is to write as clearly as possible and avoid any attempt to impress with excessive emphasis or style. If the form calls for block capitals, again clear presentation is essential but it is unlikely that any analysis is planned.

## PSYCHOLOGICAL TESTS

The use of psychological and aptitude tests runs in phases although they are consistently popular at school-leaver level. For a time, tests were thought to give answers to most hiring problems, but it is difficult to find convincing evidence that they predict success in a job, particularly at managerial level, with sufficient degree of certainty. They can give indications of temperament and personality but these must be checked out by the interviewer as it is possible to fake the tests. It would be a most unwise firm which believed in the infallibility of any testing procedure. Tests are also expensive in terms of time and so, until someone comes along with a cast-iron certain predictability, they will remain an option in recruitment procedures which only some firms will continue to exercise.

Applicants generally dislike this form of assessment and, having taken a test, you should state your feelings if asked – it can do no harm to have some sort of alibi if you have not scored well! If job hunters are faced with interviews at which tests are to be used, they can, of course, decline and say that their records are available for examination.

However, such a refusal is almost certain to mean rejection and so most people will accept the test as inescapable.

Books of aptitude tests are available in bookshops and libraries and anyone who expects to be asked to take them would be well advised to get to know the form these tests can take. Graduates will find self-administered aptitude tests of particular benefit in guiding them towards appropriate careers.

## MAKING THE BEST OF TESTS

Tests, if properly designed and used, will attempt to discover your aptitudes, strengths and weaknesses. Naturally you will want to show where your skills lie as well as building up your strong points and concealing the frailties. The problems here arise when questions are phrased in slightly differing terms so that inconsistent answers can be exposed, particularly if your responses are less than frank. This simple trap to catch the applicant who is working against the clock is by no means easy to detect.

One way to prepare yourself for tests which include these traps is to buy and use a pocket-sized thesaurus. This is a useful aid for all forms of writing as the synonyms it lists for common words help you avoid repetition. The alternatives given are usually quite simple words which often slip your mind at the vital moment; regular use of the thesaurus increases your vocabulary which in turn makes some tests easier to do. For instance, most people will be pleased to consider themselves as 'friendly' – but will they recognize all the synonyms which might appear in a personality test? The alternatives that might be offered include affectionate, amiable, amicable, auspicious, benevolent, conciliatory, cordial, favourable, fraternal, good, intimate, kind, neighbourly, peaceable, propitious, sociable, well-disposed – quite a selection! Psychological tests include, among other things, traps to test whether the candidate is being honest or merely answering in the way he thinks is wanted. This can include a number of similar questions which invite answers which may show inconsistency if faking is tried. Although all the above alternatives are not true synonyms, they all appear in the thesaurus and a test paper would expect the applicant to pick out the similar word each time. Someone who makes regular use of a thesaurus will not only develop a more interesting and wider vocabulary for general use but will also score better when faced with tests of this type.

Remember that some tests are impossible to complete in the time allowed: if you do not complete the paper, do not think this automatically means failure.

Beware of guessing at answers where you are offered alternative solutions to problems. Some tests carry penalty points for incorrect answers, making it to your disadvantage to guess. You can always ask the tester if the test you are about to take carries this penalty system.

Psychological tests may be designed to discover, among other things, what motivates you. For example:

Mark with an X the two most important reasons for working:

1. Chance to show initiative
2. Good working conditions
3. Good working companions
4. Good boss
5. Security
6. Money
7. Good hours
8. Interest in work
9. Promotion
10. Credit and recognition.

The answers desired in this test are numbers 6 and 8.

Another question might try to discover how you see yourself, for example:

Mark the words which most and least describe you:

> Persuasive
>
> Gentle
>
> Humble
>
> Original.

The test is looking for people who see themselves as 'persuasive' and reject the description of 'humble'. Further examples of tests can be found in *Selection and Assessment at Work* by G. Jessup and H. Jessup.

Above all, never underestimate tests. They may not be as useful as some people think, but obviously the company which is using them regards them as worthwhile. No company is going to appoint someone on the basis of good test results alone but, just as important, no firm is going to be happy about taking on an applicant who came across well at interview but whose test scores showed inconsistency or worse. Tests, like application forms, are another method of weeding out candidates, *not* a method of selecting them.

# 5

# Preparation for the Interview

As I pointed out in chapter 2, under conditions of high unemployment it is harder on average to get interviews than to convert interviews into job offers but, having made that statistical point, I must stress that it would be the utmost folly to waste an interview by failing to prepare thoroughly for it.

Preparing for an interview means that you research your prospective employer, you think out how you will control the interview and you ensure that everything you do projects the correct image for the job in question.

**RESEARCHING THE COMPANY**

There is simply no excuse for going to an interview, being asked 'What do you know about us?' and replying 'Little or nothing.' It is imperative that you are familiar with the company's products or services, its markets, how many people it employs, where it is based and its recent financial results. Only by knowing all that and relating it to the job you are seeking can you expect to show how valuable you could be to the firm.

Where do you find the information? There is a wide variety of sources which include: the company itself (consult its annual reports, which might be available in a local library or college, its balance sheet and its promotional material);

libraries (including the City Business Library in London); Companies' House; employees and company sales teams; competitors and their sales teams; suppliers; creditors; products; *Daily Telegraph* information services; EXTEL information cards; trade or professional associations; unions; Department of Employment; Chamber of Commerce. Public libraries keep a wealth of directories which are of considerable value to the job hunter seeking information about an organization. Your friendly librarian will be only too pleased to help you find the appropriate volume as a break from date-stamping the latest sci-fi story or romantic novel. If a particular firm is not well reported in the available directories, the library will again be glad to make enquiries on your behalf.

What do you need to know about a firm? Much depends on the job and its level, but among the things you will want to know are: ownership; finance (profit/profitability, expansion plans, cash flow); return on capital invested (well capitalized or struggling, contraction or expansion, diversification, inter-firm comparisons, rationalization, attempts at take-over, share value and trend); personnel at director level; opinions of people who know the firm (knowledge of the management and their lengths of service); past redundancies; succession plans; staff turnover record; is the job a new one? if not, what happened to the last incumbent? why no internal promotion? company organization structure; products (range, profitability, market share, problems, research and development, competition, new products, exports, new markets, rationalization of products); production (sources of raw materials, new or obsolete machinery, safety record, shift working, quality control, transport arrangements, retail or wholesale outlets); policy on public relations, advertising, marketing, personnel, finance, administration; and so on. It will not be possible to find answers to all these questions in every case and some of the information will be subjective, but the more knowledgeable you can be, the more you will impress the interviewer. The more you know and have found out, the more it will be clear that you are an applicant who wants to work for this company.

Information derived from the research can have another value; many people get jobs and then regret the move. Often comments are heard that the disillusioned employee should have taken notice of the negative signals which emerged in research or even at the interview itself. Firms which give hints of parsimony or extreme generosity coupled with other indicators may tell a story; job hunters should tune into what they see and hear to avoid a wrong move.

## QUESTIONS TO ASK

When you are offered an interview, telephone and accept the invitation (or change it as may be the case), ask who will be seeing you and then confirm the arrangements in writing. You should also enquire about the time allocated for the meeting – is it to be one hour or half a day?

Candidates are invariably invited to put questions to their interviewers and any failure to take up the offer will probably mean that you are branded as lacking in imagination or worse. Good questions are unlikely to arise out of thin air, and the successful job hunter will have prepared at least twenty points to raise before attending the interview. Write them out on paper so that interviewers can see that you have done some homework as they have done theirs. Try to plan questions for everyone who is likely to be present at the interview. Some of the points you intended to raise will already have been covered during the course of discussion, but you can always fall back on stock questions which can be put at intervals or when you are invited to do so.

Asking the interviewer to describe the short- and long-term objectives of the company will prompt a pause for thought and give you a break. Enquiring about the major problems expected in the job will allow you to bring forward points which will be of particular interest at a later stage. You may learn about new products, competition, expansion, new machinery, new staff and so on. Requests for an organization chart or, if one is offered, queries about where you would fit into it, are also good for showing that you are alert and interested. If the interviewer offers you financial information which is more up-to-date than any you could discover, ask how the next quarter's results are expected to go. Ask what happened to the person who has just vacated the job and how long he or she held the post. If the most recent incumbent only survived a few months, enquire about the predecessor.

Try to discover whether your interviewer has been with the firm a long time. The answer will help you judge any attitudes expressed and how they conform to the company's official line. It may be unwise to ask the length of service directly; lead the interviewer gently into confiding the information if you think it is worth having. Enquire about how departmental budgets are prepared and ask what freedom of action you would have in spending the money.

Try to prepare questions for each stage of the interview. For example, if there has been a discussion on recruitment, ask about future expansion plans. Job hunters who have researched their firm thoroughly will have no difficulty in raising relevant queries. However, even if the interviewer provides a wealth of information as part of an introduction, job hunters still have no problems as they can fall back as necessary on the words why, what, how, who, where and when when they want a respite. These prompts are guaranteed to get the interviewer talking – but remember to *listen* to the replies.

Naturally you will want to know what the job will bring in salary, benefits, holidays and so on. Some of this information you may know from the original advertisement or the interviewer may offer details at some stage. Much as you will want to hear about this, do not ask until late in the second interview. To ask sooner suggests that you might be overconcerned about the rewards and less keen on the responsibilities which the job carries.

## TIMING OF THE INTERVIEW

Interviewers are human and they have their good and bad days as well as their peaks and troughs in every day. Successful job hunters will want to ensure that they avoid the problem days and times, which should present no difficulties. By far the best days are in mid-week. Many people are not at their most understanding on Mondays or Fridays, so why take a risk? The best time is first thing in the morning. This sets the standard and everyone else is compared to you. Next choice is last thing in the afternoon, when you leave a lasting impression. The worst possible time is immediately after lunch – the interviewer may be weary after a liquid lunch!

If you are invited to an interview on a problem day or at a difficult time, *change it*. Telephone to confirm your interest in the post and ask for an alternative appointment. If you are worthy of an interview, no sensible firm will reject you because you ask for another time and have a fair reason for doing so. Should they offer you a choice, take the last of the days mentioned and set one of the better times so that you will leave that lasting impression.

## APPEARANCE

The self-presentation required depends on the type of employer you are applying to: for jobs in professions such as legal work, accounting or finance and industrial management, smart but conventional dress is less likely to put the employer off. But in situations where creativity and individuality are seen as vital to the job, such as the media, the fashion world and advertising, you are not so limited. The important thing is to look smart and clean and dress in a way which will be acceptable to your prospective employer – not to put him or her off by your appearance before you have had a chance to prove your ability to do the job. However much you might want to work in a casual sweater and jeans, this is not yet accepted business dress. For a man, a dark or mid-blue suit is still regarded as the norm, and if you envisage attending a number of interviews and don't own one, that could be one of your better investments. Women lack the safe choice of a conventional suit and need to take care to look neat and well-groomed without being dowdy. Heavy makeup, strong perfume and an abundance of jewellery are to be avoided; wear clothes that feel right for a busy work environment.

For men or women, any hint of shabby dress – a worn shirt collar, missing buttons, laddered tights – will do nothing for the impression you are trying to create. Many interviewers make a point of looking at the candidate's shoes to see if they were cleaned that morning – an obvious point for attention. In most cases, bow ties, dark glasses and anything which is other than conservative is out. White or blue shirts might be boring but they are still the best and safest bet for men. But in fashion or youthful environments in areas where individuality is expected, as in advertising or design work, a more extrovert appearance is expected. Some firms will automatically give women black marks for wearing trousers. Revealing dresses are equally unhelpful for those who are trying to win jobs through their skills and experience.

For a second interview, the question might arise as to whether or not a change of clothing is best. There is something to be said for showing that you have more than one suit and shirt or decent dress, but bear in mind that the way you dressed before did not put the interviewer off, so it's probably best to dress in a similar way, if not in the same clothes.

Smoking is absolutely out. Cigarettes are becoming less socially acceptable and even if your interviewer smokes or invites you to do so, decline – without stating or indicating disapproval.

Appearances count for a lot and clothes, personal grooming and attention to detail can help you look a winner. But remember: clothes will not get you a job – they can put the interviewer right off, or they can merely enhance a good impression.

## PUNCTUALITY

A company is entitled to think that if a candidate cannot arrive in time for the interview this indicates a problem with timekeeping. That may be unimportant to some, but to others it is significant. If possible, plan to arrive in the area with time in hand for a cup of coffee. If the railway or road conditions cause you to be delayed, telephone your interviewer as soon as possible when you realize you are going to be late. Explain what has happened and the interviewer will, in all probability, be prepared to await your arrival. When you get there, he or she will doubtless sympathize with you and you are off to a fair start; it's better to arrive on time, but at least you have not simply arrived late and mumbled about the traffic.

If you arrive at the premises early, take a walk around the area – it may tell you something more about the job, the company and its environment. Plan to reach the interviewer's office about five minutes before the appointed time; any earlier can be an embarrassment, any later suggests you cut things too finely.

Sometimes the interviewer will keep you waiting. If you are offered an apology and perhaps a cup of coffee, accept them gracefully. Look at any company or trade journals which are lying around – you might learn something and you will give the impression of being keen to add to your professional knowledge. If there are newspapers available, choose carefully which to read – an interest in one with the 'wrong' political viewpoint or an undue fascination with sport, sex or scandal will not help your image! If you are kept waiting for half an hour, it is quite reasonable to ask how much longer you can expect to wait. If the delay extends much beyond that, it is fair to ask if the interviewer would prefer you to make another appointment as obviously this is a very busy time.

Should it happen that you leave without having been interviewed, write to the company immediately you return home and explain that it was impossible to stay as you had another appointment or a last train to catch. Consider carefully whether or not you want to get further involved with the firm – there may be a message in what happened.

## TYPICAL QUESTIONS

Every interviewer will ask about essential things such as your duties and responsibilities in your current or previous post, and all candidates will be ready to answer such obvious questions. Job hunters must also prepare to be asked many more searching questions; it pays to have thought about how to handle the routine ones. It is unforgivable to land an interview, research the firm and then waste the chance of an offer through failure to prepare for obvious questions.

Among some of the favourite questions might be:

What are your short- and long-term career ambitions?
What is your management philosophy?
What job would you like to do if you had a completely free choice?
What are you looking for in a job?
What are typical criticisms of you in your present job?
Why do you want to move?
How long will you expect to stay with us?
How long before you expect to show results in this post?
What is special about you that makes you our ideal choice?
What salary are you expecting?
What is wrong with your present company?
How do you rate your present firm?

Define success.
What is your health record?
Can you stand pressure? Give an example.
What is your greatest failing?
What is your strongest attribute?
How have you changed the nature of your present job?
Why have you not obtained a job so far?
Why aren't you earning more at your age?
What are your five greatest achievements so far?
Why did you only get a third-class degree? (or certificate, etc.)
Do you prefer line or service management posts?
What objectives have you set yourself in your present job?
What do you think of your boss?
What interests you most/least about the job you have applied for?
What do you like/dislike most about your present job?
Describe your own personality.
Are you creative? Give an example.
Are you analytical? Give an example.
Are you a good manager? Give an example.
Are you a good leader? Give an example.
How have you increased sales/productivity?
Why do you want to leave your present firm?
How have you reduced costs?
Have you fired people?
Have you hired people? What do you look for?
What do your staff think of you?
Why do you want to work for us?
If you had the chance to work for any employer in the country, who would you choose? Why?
What other jobs are in the pipeline?
Why do you think you have top management potential?
Describe yourself to us in three minutes.
How much do you know about us?
How do your colleagues see you?

Do you lose your temper?
Where will you be in five and ten years' time?
What books/magazines/newspapers do you read?
What are your spare-time activities?
Are you a good team player?
Are you a loner?
What questions would you ask if you were in my chair?

The serious job hunter will write out answers to all the above questions and the many others which they will inspire. Never learn the answers off by heart, but if you think through these points it will be much easier to respond when the interviewer puts the questions than if you face them unprepared.

In the case of people who seek jobs as technicians, such as toolmakers, the evidence of their employability is their work and the reputation of their employers. In the case of managers, their skills are much harder to define and even a full interview will not reveal all the views and attitudes which make up their personality. The best that you can hope for as an interviewee is to project yourself in positive ways; by thinking about the questions listed above and the answers you would give, you can choose interesting words to describe everyday matters. In other words, you can *sell* yourself in an honest but attractive manner.

Obviously I cannot offer an appropriate list of answers as all applicants will have their own tales to tell, but I will give some guidance concerning your approach to presentation of your answers.

Much of the question-and-answer process is a psychological battle, and the detailed answer can often be less important than the thinking which might lie behind it. For example, it is essential to have an acceptable reason for wanting to leave your last job, and probably the one before that, but there is not much wrong in admitting to having made a mistake when you joined the wrong firm ten years earlier. Naturally, you were too young to spot the dangers but now, looking back, you are wise enough to see the error! Certainly, you have no criticism of your present firm. If you are unemployed, remember that it was the job, not the person, which was declared redundant.

You will nearly always be asked to state your greatest strengths and weaknesses and you should think this one out in advance. There is nothing to be said against a little mild self-praise provided it is not overdone; to decline to answer is modesty taken too far. There will be many areas where you are strong – choose your reply to fit the particular situation. It would, on the other hand, be arrogant to claim no weaknesses so the skill is to answer with a point which is to many people not a weakness but a virtue. For example, you might admit to being unable to suffer fools gladly, which may well gain you some plus marks.

Other answers might be along the following lines:

'How long do you plan to stay with us?'

'I'm looking for a career opportunity and, as long as you are happy with me, I'll remain while I can advance my career. I hope that will be a considerable length of time.'

'How long before you would expect to show results in this post?'

'I hope I will be contributing in a very short time, but it will take me some time to find out how things work in this organization. Once I know my way around, I believe that my past experience can quickly be put to use.'

'What do you think of your boss?'

'He's a first-class man and I have learned a lot from him. I have enjoyed working with him and my colleagues.'

'Why do you want to leave your present firm?'

'I'm keen to find additional responsibility and earn more money. I want to add to my experience and, because I see no openings in my present firm in the foreseeable future, I have to look elsewhere.'

'Where do you see yourself in five or ten years' time?'

'That depends on the job I accept and the company I join. I am not too concerned about job titles but more interested in an enjoyable and rewarding position. My five and ten year plans will depend on the responsibility I am given.'

'What are your spare-time activities?'

'I have a wide range of interests, though the demands of work and family life oblige me to limit them, but I particularly enjoy practical activities and have converted my attic into a playroom. I am also a member of my local Round Table which can involve many different people and needs.'

'Are you a good team player or a loner?'

'My record shows that I have achieved results in previous jobs which could not have been realized without teamwork, and my ability to motivate my staff shows in our achievements. At the same time, I know that the manager of any department must take decisions based on the best information available, and this sometimes requires one to act alone. Any decisions must then be properly communicated to all those concerned.'

'What questions would you ask if you were in my chair?'

'This has been a very interesting discussion, and you have covered everything I would expect you to ask about. The only question left is to ask me if I am still interested in the appointment, and I most certainly am.'

At some stage of the interview the interviewer will almost certainly bring up the question of money and ask you what salary you are seeking in your next job. If this happens early in the discussions, try to stall by saying something like 'I *am* interested in the job, but can we defer the matter of salary until later?' If pressed, give your reason for delay as 'I'd like to hear more about the job and responsibilities first' – it is unlikely that any interviewer would quarrel with that. However, there is always the exception and if you are unable to escape with what has been suggested so far, the next ploy is to turn the tables and ask the interviewer 'What is the salary range for the job?' That should ease the pressure momentarily; the interviewer might answer 'The planned salary is within the range of £15,00 to £18,000.' Your response should be to look pleased and say 'I am looking for £18,000 (top of bracket) to £20,000.' If all your efforts to move the conversation in this direction fail and you are forced into stating your salary requirements, quote a salary bracket which encompasses a 'fair' rate for the job.

If you are redundant, you can expect to be asked why it has taken you so long to find work. When you answer, stress your desire to find the *right* job, not just any post, and point out that meanwhile your time has been filled with consultancy work, further education, writing or whatever. You may be accused of being too old or too young; your response must be a suitably light-hearted protest that there is no such thing! Age has advantages and disadvantages in terms of training, experience and attitude – choose whatever applies to your case to debate the point.

Too long a time spent with any organization can count against you, particularly if the period includes the vital time from around thirty to the mid-forties when career advancement should be taking place if it is going to happen at all. If you can show that you have progressed within a firm this will partly mitigate the problem, but do give this question serious thought in advance. Too short a time with an organization can also be an embarrassment. If the company ran into difficulties and was obliged to contract, say so; otherwise it may be possible to gloss over very short engagements by 'losing' them on your c.v.

Interviews are occasions when questions will come thick and fast. It would be an ill-prepared candidate who did not rehearse answers to the more obvious points and who gave no thought to what intention lies behind the questions.

## PROBLEMS WOMEN FACE

In recent years, legislation has been enacted which tries to correct the unfairness that has prevented women entering many industries and jobs, as well as lowering barriers which affected social activities. Nevertheless, discrimination against women still exists in the business world and it is idle to pretend otherwise. The problem will only be resolved over many years as attitudes change; at present women applicants must expect to face additional hurdles in their career quest. Prejudice still remains, although it may not be openly voiced and, particularly for women returning to a career after a gap of some years, it is important to consider some of the common additional difficulties which might be met at interview; male chauvinism, sexual intimidation and male condescension are still found, but the more common difficulties arise from employers' concerns about the extent of women's commitment to careers. They often feel that domestic matters will take up more of women's time than men's.

The problems will very much depend on the profession or trade you are involved in, but individual interviewers may have prejudices in any field. It is essential that you prepare yourself for the most common questions. Decide whether you are prepared to work for an employer who asks you whether you intend to have children, whether you intend to get married soon, or why you don't stay at home with the kids. If you are (and most women at present unfortunately still have to be), you will at some point have to answer these and other questions, so think out your views and be prepared to state them calmly and with confidence. A woman who is upset or seething with rage and uncertain how to respond will not impress the interviewer. If your interviewer is a woman, don't assume that she will be 'on your side'. She may well ask all the usual questions.

The 'male chauvinist pig' mentality operates on the assumption that women are only suited to certain types of work. Any anger which you might feel against this kind of interviewer must not be shown, as it only exacerbates the problem – the interviewer will only conclude that women are, as he suspected, 'too emotional' for a business appointment. While it is possible to bring a charge on the grounds of sexual discrimination, that will neither get you the job, nor change attitudes. Women can of course change attitudes, but generally only after they take up their posts.

Almost all women are liable, at some time, to be 'tested' by men who will try to bring sexual innuendo into business discussions. Women can, in that situation, only maintain a cool, polite response. Again, you can protest, but to do so will jeopardize your chance of the job, or promotion if the advances are from a colleague. No self-respecting man or woman will operate like that, but it does happen. An organization which knows it is going on and turns a blind eye is not a fit place for anyone to work. I have already stressed the importance of dressing appropriately, and a professional and businesslike appearance will help dissuade the interviewer from any unprofessional remarks.

A male interviewer will sometimes try to undermine a female applicant with remarks like 'Surely you would rather be looking after the family than worrying about market share?' It seems not to occur to such men that women are unlikely, unless forced by financial problems, to apply for a job they do not want. Fulfilment at work is just as important to women as men, and you can quickly put the interviewer right by telling him so in a polite but cool manner. Sometimes these questions are put deliberately to test reactions; a hard-headed business woman should not be intimidated by them.

Male interviewers, and some female ones, will often take more interest in a woman's marital status than they would in a man's. The firm will reason that a married woman is more likely to move because her husband moves than vice versa, and it is concerned about the cost of recruitment if this should happen within a short time. You should consider your answers to questions on this subject carefully before the interview.

One of the most common questions young married women face is whether they intend to have children. Employers don't want the costs of maternity leave and/or re-recruitment. Think about your answer in advance: a good answer would be along the lines of: 'I have no immediate plans to have children, and am fully committed to my career for the foreseeable future.' Employers cannot reasonably expect you to swear that you will never have children; depending on the level of the job you are applying for they are unlikely to expect the successful candidate to stay more than five years in any case. The basic point to get over is your continuing commitment to your job. Tempting though it may be, don't mention that the question is only legal if it has also been put to male candidates unless you have already decided against the job. Then give that as one of your reasons for declining, and you may have done something to change their future practice.

A woman who has children can expect her interviewer to ask about how they will be looked after. Men are never asked these questions unless they are single parents. This is unfair, but while women continue to bear more day-to-day responsibility for children than men, employers will be worried about their possible absence because of children's illnesses etc. In jobs which require absence from home overnight this will be a particular problem. Have your answer ready: if you have made arrangements for the care of the children and are satisfied that they are adequate you can convey your confidence to the interviewer and eliminate this as a reason for not offering you the job.

More people are now living together without going through a wedding ceremony than ever before. A single woman may escape questions about her home life, although she may be just as committed to her partner as her married counterpart. In most fields it would be unwise to volunteer the information that you are living with a man, but unmarried to him. There is almost certainly a double standard on this matter, as a man in such a position is seldom the subject of adverse comment, but if you are really keen to get a job in a rather conservative trade or profession it will be easier if you avoid the subject. With plenty of people to choose from, most selectors will opt for the conventional candidate, and the area remains a minefield.

Employers above all else want to hire people who have clear goals in line with their own and work towards them. Women can lose out if they wear their femininity as a badge or a wound, if they over-stress family considerations, overdo makeup, perfume, or jewellery, or dress in a way which suggests they are more interested in catching the eye than demonstrating their ability to fill a post. Employers are interested in drive, ability and achievements in the person they want to appoint. If a woman can demonstrate these, and point, where relevant, to cost reductions, sales records, new products and other benefits which she can bring to her new employer, she will be in a strong position.

Some women will suffer considerable handicaps in their careers just because they are female, and this is grossly unfair. In any job, women will frequently feel that they have to be better than a man just to survive, and the old prejudices are very slowly breaking down. Confidence in your own ability, and unflappability in the face of questioning about your domestic concerns, are the best approaches: don't show resentment unless you don't want the job. There are many helpful publications about women's rights and sexual discrimination; see the list of publications at the end of this book.

# 6
# The Interview

Everything you have done so far will be wasted if you fail to convert the interview into an offer of employment. Interview preparation is vital but, to make it pay off, you must consider and plan your interview behaviour equally carefully.

If you have followed the advice in this book you will turn up at the interview neatly dressed, on time and well prepared. You will know that your earlier contacts with the company will have set you apart and your interviewer will be keen to find out if you measure up to expectation.

Interviews should not be conducted on a parent – child model but as discussions between equals. That does not always happen, which can be attributed to the interviewer or interviewee adopting an unhelpful role towards the other person. The job hunter can avoid the risk of such an imbalance by taking control of the situation from the outset without the interviewer realizing it.

Avoid appearing subservient; you should aim to appear as a learned, charming and diplomatic individual who is socially acceptable and moderately outgoing without being overbearing. Give the right impression from the start by greeting the interviewer with a friendly smile and firm handshake. Limp or vice-like grips should not influence a truly professional interviewer but at this stage his or her competence cannot be gauged, and so your first contact has to be right. Be ready to return the interviewer's greeting with your own 'Good morning, Mr Green. How do you do?' It is important to use the interviewer's name as he or she will use yours – everyone likes to think that other people care enough to get names right.

Most interviewers will immediately try to set candidates at ease with some small talk, but there may be a point to win for the job hunter who takes the initiative and offers some remark about the weather or the state of the roads or, if the worst has happened, makes an apology for late arrival. By doing this you will have shown that you have confidence in yourself and are perfectly at ease. You are ready for the situation and the interviewer has been relieved of the problem of dealing with a nervous applicant.

## SETTING THE SCENE

A well-organized interviewer will have ensured that you have been properly received in the outer office and your coat has been taken from you. When you enter the inner office, you should be carrying no more than a document case or handbag. Wait until you are invited to sit down. If you have not been relieved of your coat, you should ask if there is somewhere you should put it rather than risk throwing it over the interviewer's favourite chair! There may be a second person in the room to interview you. Try to angle your chair towards the lead interviewer if that person can be identified.

Don't attend an interview carrying a large briefcase – interviewers may interpret it as an attempt to intimidate them. Always have some material with you, even if it is just your prepared list of questions; a document case makes the ideal impression, provided it is not overflowing.

Never put anything on the interviewer's desk. That is personal territory and you must not appear to encroach upon it. Even a coffee cup should be kept in your hand unless someone has put it on the desk for you or the interviewer has offered a few square inches for you to use. Never risk putting a wet cup down on a polished surface – ask for a mat or something to avoid marking the desk. Your consideration will earn you another plus point.

## DOS AND DON'TS

Always try to phrase your responses in positive terms, avoiding the use of negatives. It makes for easier understanding and presents you as more of an optimist than a pessimist. Much scorn is heard at the expense of the British tendency to discuss the weather, but it is a useful opener at an interview. Even at this stage let your positive view of life show; don't grumble at the weather, but try to put the positive point of view!

Speak at a normal, controlled pace; many people talk too quickly, especially when they are nervous, so you may need to make a special attempt to slow down.

Always understate your need for the job – make the firm want you, but be careful to avoid playing hard-to-get too convincingly. When the interviewer begins to sell you the job, you are on the way!

Don't put up with indignities: if you find yourself faced with an interviewer who is rude, ask yourself if this is the kind of firm you ought to be considering. If the answer is no, close the interview politely and start thinking about the next one. Rudeness could be deliberate as part of a stress interview – see below, page 84.

At all times, keep the job in question in mind and phrase your replies to suit the particular requirements of the appointment. Try to project an image of sincerity, achievement and enthusiasm, and avoid becoming over-serious. A little light aside and the occasional smile as you answer a question can go a long way to showing you are a human being and not just a machine.

Watch out for the accidental or deliberate silence. The interviewer may be giving you the chance to put your foot in it by adding to a previous answer in some unhelpful way or waiting to see if you will break the silence with some ill-considered remark. If a gap does appear in the interview and the silence becomes awkward, this is the time to put one of your prepared questions, but not just any question. Ask something which shows that you have done your homework, such as 'I see that your half-yearly report shows an increase in sales turnover of 20 per cent from last year – will that be maintained over the full year?' If this gets a simple 'Yes' or 'No', the next question should be 'What is the reason for that?' In addition to demonstrating your knowledge, you have given yourself some respite from the interviewer's barrage of questions and can catch your breath.

Do make the odd complimentary remark about the firm. It should not be overdone and must be based on fact rather than empty comment.

Listen attentively to what is said to you. It looks bad if you ask about something your interviewer has just told you. Use information which is given to you to write a good follow-up letter and ask intelligent questions. To request people to expand on points they have just made makes them feel they have succeeded in catching your interest. How can they think that you are anything but an intelligent person?

If you are asked a question which is ambiguous, ask for clarification rather than risk answering the wrong point. It shows commendable caution and that you try to get things clear before you act. If you do not know the answer to a question, say so. To waffle on when it is obvious that you are talking nonsense is much more damaging than to say something like: 'I don't know the answer to that one. It's an area I hope to learn more about.'

Be aware of the risk of 'talking down' to the interviewer. Personnel managers are unlikely to know too many details about technical matters but you should assume that they understand unless they say otherwise. They can always stop you if they want to, which is better than making them feel inferior if you were foolish enough to say 'You may not be familiar with the technology so please say if I am leaving you behind.' Beware of being better than the people interviewing you. Despite what they might claim, managers are unlikely to hire someone who might be a threat to them. Wait until you get the job before you let the firm see who should be in the boss's chair!

Angle your answers to show how you can help the firm. The company is not interested in employing you for your sake but because you can meet its needs. You must show your interviewer that you recognize this and that you can deliver the goods.

A professional interviewer will work to a framework, probably that described by Alec Rodger in *The Seven Point Plan* (National Institute of Industrial Psychology), which ensures that all vital areas are covered. If this does not happen, you may need to guide the interview gently to prevent it deteriorating into an aimless chat. I have provided a very brief outline of the Seven Point Plan at the end of this book. Only amateur job hunters would risk being ignorant of it.

If lunch out is part of the procedure, let your interviewer choose first and be guided on price. Avoid sloppy foods – a stain on your shirt or blouse does not fit the image you want to present. Limit your drinks to the absolute minimum – one glass of wine and a sherry are enough to meet the social niceties while preventing an overloose tongue. Anything more gives the impression that you are more than a social drinker and will count against you.

Don't try to read what is on the interviewer's desk, play with your watch or jewellery, fiddle with your fingers or rings or otherwise do things which distract.

Avoid topics which invite trouble – religion, politics and race are forbidden territory, unless, of course, the appointment is in the Church, or concerns political matters or race relations. Don't name-drop. Your interviewer may well have been given the cold shoulder by the person whose name you have used, which will not help your cause.

Don't be smothered under an avalanche of questions posed so quickly that you have no chance to answer one before the next comes along. If your interviewer tries that tactic, wait for the end and then say 'You have asked quite a number of separate questions there; let me answer the first one.' Answer the question and if you still hold the floor, ask the interviewer to repeat the next point. Trying to remember and answer ten questions in a row means that you will be talking too long and might bore your listener. The solution is to pass the responsibility back; if the interviewer really wants to raise a particular issue, this is the chance to revive it.

Throughout the interview you must avoid arguing with the interviewer. Your responses should convey enthusiasm, be factual (showing you know your subject and job), and visual (an animated expression is needed). Simple 'Yes' or 'No' answers are acceptable in response to certain questions but, on the whole, detailed statements will be expected from you. A good interviewer knows how to ask questions which will call forth full answers, but if that is not happening it is up to you to assist. Do not repeat questions in the answers.

Never try to answer a question until the interviewer has stopped talking – it is bad manners and suggests that you jump into action before getting all the facts.

Don't let your answers go on for too long. Watch for signs of boredom in the interviewer, and keep to the point. If more detail is wanted, it will be asked for in a further question. Have you been guilty of making your listener feel weary? Ask a question – a good way of waking people up again.

Even if interviewers introduce themselves by their first names and use yours, they tend, curiously, to be less than pleased if you address them by theirs! 'Mr Green' is the safest bet, although your interviewer may then tell you to 'Call me Reg'; even then, the best tactic is to avoid using any name if possible. Male interviewees should not remove their jackets unless invited to do so, even if their interviewer is casually dressed.

Avoid qualifying statements such as 'I think. . .', 'I

believe. . .', 'If my memory serves me right. . .', and others of that type. They serve no purpose and quickly irritate the listener. The habit of stringing everything together with 'and' and 'but' should also be avoided. Beware of the 'ums' and 'ers' which pollute speech. Phrases such as 'you know' and 'you see' can cause great annoyance – if you think your interviewer is beginning to count the number of times you use them rather than listen to what you are saying, you have problems!

Never lie at an interview. Lies are hard to remember and usually find you out. However, that is not to say that you are obliged to tell the *whole* truth: if the interviewer doesn't follow up a potentially dangerous question, it is not your job to volunteer information which will damage you. If you have particularly weak areas, you will have to think the problem through and develop your own truthful answers which present you in the best possible light in the circumstances.

Don't give details away about your present employer. If you let your interviewer think that confidential information is unsafe with you, your chance of a new job has gone.

## MONEY

If your interview has gone well, salary is likely to be discussed towards the end of the first meeting or certainly at a second interview. The responses I suggested above are recommended for dealing with money matters if they are raised early on, but there will be a point at which serious negotiations have to take place.

Some industries and firms are well-known low payers – you will probably know which. You may glean details about the organization you are visiting during the interview, or the original advertisement, if you saw one, may have mentioned a salary range. Most companies know what they are going to pay to fill a post even when they advertise a salary as 'negotiable'. Only if you are being head-hunted or are fortunate enough to have a company 'making' a job for you will there really be a chance to agree on something out of the ordinary.

A job might have a salary range of £14,000 to £18,000, or 30 per cent over the minimum. The probability is that the firm will try to fill the job at the lowest possible figure, but in practice they will be willing to go up to about the mid-point of the salary range. In my example, this means that an applicant can expect to negotiate from £14,000 to £16,000.

To make negotiations meaningful, the applicant must ask for the current salary range of the appointment and not be fobbed off with a reply which only quotes the range to be paid on first appointment.

If your present income is relatively low, you will not want to disclose it too early before the company has had a chance to think about your qualities. Any allowances which you enjoy should be quoted to bolster your earnings because your new employer will certainly try to evaluate your potential worth in terms of your current income. You may be tempted to inflate your present earnings but you should resist it – exaggerations are relatively easily discovered if the firm checks with your previous employers (once you have left them, they may be less confidential about such matters than you would hope), or your P45 or P60 could give your game away.

If you are unemployed, there will be pressure on you to accept almost any salary. But the job hunter who is moving on for financial or career reasons should be looking for an increase of around 15 per cent to 25 per cent at least. The cost of moving may be partly reimbursed by your new employer but there are many extras which cannot be recovered and a meagre salary increase can soon disappear. To move for a trifling increase is hard to justify and may need some explanation in the future to interviewers who suspect that the move was forced rather than freely chosen.

Before trying to negotiate terms, you must be certain that the appointment is going to be offered. Once the job has been offered and accepted, if things have been well handled, the precise salary can be discussed. Bad timing or over-eagerness to talk money might wreck the deal and the age-old British reticence about money must be faced. There is nothing to be said for accepting the employers' suggestion that they will write and confirm the job is yours and state the salary they are ready to pay at the same time. This leaves you in a losing position; either you accept the job as offered, or say 'No, unless. . .'. The outcome of the latter course might be the withdrawal of the job except on the original terms offered, or more likely the job will be offered to the second choice.

If you are the only person who can do the job and you have been head-hunted you are in a strong position, but it is likely that there will be someone in the wings. This runner-up may be equally able to fill the vacancy, even at a lower price, so you cannot push too hard. Prudence is your only guide; if you think you have a job offer in your hands, you must judge the situation as well as you can and accept the offer if you think asking for more will count against you.

In any negotiation, it is advantageous to try and communicate your thinking rather than conjure numbers out of the air. Your future employers will see your reasoning and if yours is a strong case, it will help them to see and meet your goals. It is usually better to talk of a percentage increase over your last salary — the figures sound lower than if you talk of thousands of pounds extra.

If an offer is made at the interview, always ask for time to consider it. The employer has thought about it and so you are only asking for equal opportunity to think it over and perhaps discuss it with your family. If the firm wants you and has made you a definite offer, it is not going to withdraw it if you need to discuss the details with others who will be affected. It is up to your personal judgement whether you try to improve the offer when you return with your answer, but apart from clarifying minor points of detail, this is not recommended.

Discussion might turn to the prospects for the future if the salary offer falls slightly short of your expectations; a promise of a review in three or six months instead of a year could be a way to reach agreement. Better help with removal costs can be another method of improving your benefits and others include life insurance, private medical plan, company car and petrol, share purchase scheme, company purchase of your existing house, discounts on company goods and profit-sharing or bonus schemes. Taxation may affect some parts of the package and this needs to be considered too.

When the final deal is struck, you should show your delight with the excitement of a new challenge, the firm and the future and give your new employers every reason to feel that they have gained a valuable new member for their team.

A successful job hunter will also be a successful negotiator, neither being ready to concede defeat nor trying to inflict it on the new employer. If things are sensitively handled, the final offer can be a handsome advance on the initial one without your making the employers feel they have been taken beyond their fair limit.

## CLOSING TECHNIQUES

If the interview has gone on long enough and you have achieved the objective of selling yourself in the best possible way, help to end the meeting if the interviewer seems unable to do so. Your interviewer may be showing signs of having covered all the necessary ground and answered your questions, and may be shuffling papers around, trying to end the interview. Take the hint: gather together your own papers of questions and research material plus any other items which you have brought or been given.

An important stage has now arrived. You want to know how the interview has gone and you also have a final chance to clear up any misunderstandings which the interviewer may have picked up during the discussions, a possibility which you cannot allow to pass uncorrected. In some circumstances, you may be able to tackle the situation head-on by looking your interviewer straight in the eye and speaking out clearly: 'I have enjoyed our discussion, the job interests me and my experience seems to suit your needs. Have I been able to meet your requirements for the post?' Such straight talk is not always possible and can be counter-productive. You will still want some feedback from the interviewer, so a 'softer' approach may be advisable.

Again, look at your interviewer and say something like: 'I have enjoyed the opportunity of discussing this job and my potential contribution to the company. However, if there are any gaps, I would like to be told, so that I can try to answer your doubts.' Most interviewers will come up with something. You should then respond by thanking your interviewer for mentioning the point and briefly resell your relevant qualities. Continue to ask whether there are other points until no more are offered.

Having filled any gaps and corrected any misunderstandings that are raised, you finally want to know where you stand, and should say something along the lines of: 'I appreciate that you have other people to see before filling this post, but I would welcome any comments you can give me on the strength of my application.' Interviewers will often try to sidestep this question by saying that they have other people to see and therefore cannot answer. All you can do is smile in an understanding way and remind the hirer that you are asking for comments on your application – but handle this very carefully as there is a risk of doing damage instead of offering final supportive information to your interviewer.

It is more than likely that an interviewer will have decided whether to shortlist or reject you towards the end of the interview, and it does not seem unreasonable that you should be told the position. If, as may sometimes be the case, there is genuine uncertainty on the part of the interviewer, there seems nothing wrong in saying so. Traditional British reticence is out of place in what, until this final moment, should have been a frank exchange of information, but don't force a reply if you sense it will do damage.

Unfortunately, there will also be interviewers who will reply 'No problems' when they mean 'No offer'. Such a lack of honesty is particularly reprehensible when it concerns a point which the applicant could have cleared up and, perhaps, opened the way to a job offer, but once the interviewer has made up his or her mind nothing can be gained by trying to prolong the interview.

Now it is time to depart. Thank the interviewer for his or her interest, ask when you can expect to hear a decision, shake hands firmly, *smile* and say a simple 'Goodbye'. Then go. Save any curses or whoops of joy until you are well out of earshot!

## OTHER TYPES OF INTERVIEW

The one-to-one formal interview is still the most common approach but there are certain common variations.

### Trial by telephone

In these days of costly travel and even costlier overnight accommodation, some applicants are finding themselves being interviewed by telephone as the firm, or more usually a recruitment agency, responds to a written application by phoning the job hunter.

The telephone is an intrusive piece of apparatus and, sadly, Alexander Graham Bell, its inventor, failed to build into it any social manners. The result is that the wretched thing will ring at the most inopportune moments without any warning and suddenly, from engaging in the most relaxing past-times, the receiver of the call can find him or herself in a concentrated discussion with a potential employer or his agent. It can be most disconcerting and, if badly handled, can end your interest in a good job.

So what can be done to prevent a lost opportunity?

It is not the objective of this book to tell anyone how to answer the telephone properly but just stop and think of your own reaction when you call someone to be greeted with a gruff ''Ullo' – it can be off-putting. So, if a job opportunity is not to be thrown away from a bad first impression, a clear and courteous answer is needed. Most people like to be answered by the number of the person called and, if wrong, that avoids further confusion. Younger children who cannot really take in a request by a strange caller to speak to someone else should be dissuaded from grabbing the phone when it rings until they can answer it intelligently – and that means more than placing the instrument on a table without a word of explanation while young Johnny or Abigail trots off to find an adult.

The job hunter must now deal with the caller and, if possible, the call should be taken in private and certainly not against a background of television or screaming children. Again, family discipline needs to be firm when a call of this type comes through.

It takes time to gather one's wits and answer the kind of questions which a recruitment agent will ask. You must remember that, as in a face to face interview, you are trying to sell yourself and must have control of the situation. A stumble at this stage will be just as damaging as at any other interview.

So how do you get it right?

Serious job hunters will have a file on the posts in which they have an active interest together with a copy of the advertisement which first attracted them. The obvious thing to do is to have that information easily available beside the phone so that you don't have to say to the caller 'I can't exactly recall the details of the job you are discussing so can you run through it with me please.' That suggests that you might be applying for jobs without much thought as to which is the right one for you and is a certain thumbs down.

Instead, you should be able to turn up the file on that job

which will include, as well as the advertisement, a copy of your response or a least a note of the points from your standard resume which you stressed in your application and any information you have gathered on the firms so far. With that to hand, you are in a position to have an intelligent and well-focused conversation with the caller which will let him or her see that you are in control of the situation.

A call which ends with the caller thanking you for speaking to him but regretting that he does not think you are quite the type his client is seeking means that your telephone technique has room for improvement. Next time, think how you can best present your strong points and highlight the qualities which satisfy the main requirements of the job, then rehearse how to put that across succinctly. A second, personal interview is likely to be the reward for the necessary homework.

Most people find it harder to talk to someone on the phone than face to face and the level of concentration needed is very much higher when you are forced to rely on just one of your senses, hearing, instead of having the supporting sense of sight to help you through. Selling yourself by phone is hard but it has one great advantage to the serious job hunter – you will have thought it through as few of your competitors will have done and their failure to do so will have ruled them out of the next stage in the selection process. But never forget, phone calls are like application forms: they only de-select, people. No one ever gets the job as a result of one of them – the real test is the interview itself.

### Informal chat

There may be no particular job under discussion but the job hunter, by one means or another, has obtained an invitation to 'come in and chat things over'. In that situation the interviewer might open the conversation by asking the job hunter to 'tell me about yourself'. Avoid the temptation to launch into a half-hour monologue; start your reply 'I am interested in the company because. . .', and then take a maximum of two minutes to explain how your experience could be beneficial to the firm. This should open up various avenues which the interviewer may develop with your encouragement.

Another approach may be necessary if the interviewer does not offer such an invitation, and so it falls to you to say 'I'm looking forward to learning a bit more about the organization. . .' and go on to sell yourself, again keeping the time down to about two minutes. In either case you will want to channel the conversation along your chosen path. Make sure you get around to asking 'As you have no specific opening at present, what area in your company could you see me fitting into?'

## Stress interview

This is similar to cross-examination and used where it is thought necessary to force the interviewee to say something which might otherwise be held back. It is characterized by deliberate and frequent interruptions, critical comments on answers, repeated questions on specific points, extended silences and a hostile attitude.

Some interviewers think that they have to be offensive if they are to do their job well and even go as far as to tell candidates that they are not worth their present salary. There are only two ways to deal with this type of person: either tell your interrogator that you did not realize you had been invited to visit a Star Chamber and that you have better things to do, then leave; or stay cool and answer the points in a logical, calm manner. The choice depends on individual character and on your need for the job.

To allow yourself to be intimidated and pushed into apologizing for your record is completely unnecessary. Seeming to be an appeaser will not get you the job nor the respect which you would need to do it. Interviewers who use this technique are telling job hunters one thing – theirs is not the type of firm to work for.

## Panel interview

Sometimes a group of people will interview candidates at the same time. Usually they get in each other's way, often causing chaos as they all try to get their questions in without worrying about the fact that they are not developing a line of questioning or, in some cases, even listening to what has already been said. It can be very difficult to present yourself properly in such interviews as there will be scant opportunity to pursue a theme. By pure chance you may cover someone's question before it is put and, without knowing it, steal that interviewer's thunder and perhaps forfeit his or her support.

Panel interviews are particularly popular in public appointments such as teaching and local government, where everyone wants to get in on the act and no one appears to hold complete authority for selecting candidates. The system usually requires all the candidates to be interviewed on the same day when everyone on the panel has arranged to be present. Applicants are often invited for interview at the same time and so there is no leeway for arranging a more desirable appointment.

The candidates are expected to sit in the same waiting room and are called for interview in a random order, one at a time. After being interviewed, the interviewees are obliged to wait until everyone has been seen.

After the last person has been interviewed there can be a long wait while the panel makes its choice. The successful candidate is called back into the interview room and offered the post. An immediate assent is required; otherwise, in all probability, the offer will be withdrawn and offered to the second choice.

One member of the panel will then be dispatched to tell the unsuccessful applicants that the appointment has been offered and accepted by one of their number. They are then dismissed with mutterings about 'All good candidates. . . can only be one appointee. . . thank you for coming. . .'.

This is a particularly poor and often rushed method of interviewing which often fails to get beyond superficialities and leaves candidates feeling that they were denied the opportunity to do themselves justice. It sometimes also leaves the impression that the successful candidate had been chosen already, the interviews being little more than a pretence, particularly if an internal applicant gets the job.

In panel interviews, it is even more important that job hunters plan carefully how they will control events and sell themselves. Every question must be answered in a positive way which promotes the applicant's abilities and achievements. You should try to reply directly to the person who puts a question, glancing at others from time to time to show that you have not forgotten that they are there. Of course, successful job hunters will know that a panel interview awaits them and will have questions for each of the expected panel members.

When you return to the waiting room, it is not in your interest to discuss your experience with the other candidates – why give them hints which might lead to their success at your expense?

## REFERENCES

Many employers will ask you for the names of people who will give you a reference, and this must be delicately handled. It is generally safest to withhold names until you are certain to be offered the job, and at that point you must ensure that any contact with your current employer will not be made without your explicit consent. The normal practice in some jobs, such as teaching, is to request references at the first stage, and this has to be accepted.

The people you name will be those who know your recent work record, either as employer or client. Graduates can nominate employers from part-time or vacation work as well as their personal tutors or supervisors. In all cases, it is essential that you give advance warning to those you want to name, and it helps to tell them about the job so that their thoughts are focused in the right direction. Warn them that they may be telephoned rather than written to. Don't give out the names of your referees too easily or they will tire of too frequent enquiries.

Choose the titles of the people you use carefully. Someone whose title is Managing Director is going to be more impressive than a Sales Manager. If you know any, references from MPs, senior military ranks and people who hold top positions in universally-known companies are to be preferred to the owner of a little company in a back street somewhere.

References should not be major hurdles in job hunting but it would be careless to let yourself down with badly chosen referees.

## SUMMING IT UP

Over the span of their careers, serious job hunters will become accomplished at the interview game. They may quickly discover what an interviewer wants and learn to tailor their presentation to suit the circumstances. The pace of a discussion can indicate what is going on in an interviewer's mind, and it becomes easy to tell whether someone is taking an interest in your replies.

Sometimes it will become clear during an interview that this is not the job for you – but that is no reason to give up. Perhaps your skills could be of use elsewhere in the organization? Maybe creating the right impression on this occasion will lead to a future opportunity for a more interesting vacancy?

If you are unemployed, the offer of a less than marvellous job presents problems. To take or not to take the first offer can be a tricky decision, as I mentioned in chapter 2. There can be no universal answer, but perhaps thinking about why people work and reviewing your priorities might help you reach a decision.

## The Interview

Sadly, a very large proportion of interviewers are extraordinarily bad at the job. Some of them will be personnel staff who ought to be better and should have little excuse. A common difficulty occurs when the interviewer is an executive who is not accustomed to recruitment interviewing, and you need to understand the problem and make allowances. A good interviewee will spot the trouble and help the discussion along, thus gaining the grateful if unspoken thanks of the interviewer. That could help you win the job.

It is tempting to judge a firm by the standard of its interviewer. This would not be entirely fair, although a firm which allows its staff to use stress techniques is adopting a policy which may cause applicants reasonably to turn down job offers from them. Take the firm's reputation and your other knowledge of it into account; don't let one person put you off a company which is otherwise attractive.

No matter how good an interviewee you become, you will not succeed in being offered all the jobs for which you are interviewed. You will lose out because you spoke too little or too much, too loudly or too softly. Your interviewer may have taken an instant dislike to you or you may have asked for too big a salary. You can't win them all.

If you study and use the techniques described in this book, you will not be rejected because your appearance is substandard, because you present your career details in an uninteresting way, because your record is weak and poorly explained since you failed to think it through in advance, because you fail to show interest in the firm and research it badly, because you do not communicate your strengths well enough, or because you neglect to demonstrate your achievements and how they relate to the job in question. In every case the guidance given here will help make you a successful job hunter who will be two steps ahead of the field even if you start off less well qualified than the competition.

# 7

# After the Interview

After an interview, first, second or milk-round, most people consider that the procedure is complete and all they have to do is wait for the result. Why? You have worked hard, you may have travelled many miles to attend an interview, and you have undergone considerable mental strain over a concentrated period of one or two hours. Other candidates will have had similar experience to offer the employer but you want your application and interview to stand out and get you the job. The obvious course of action is to do something to remind them that you were different. There is only one thing you can do at this stage – write to the firm within forty-eight hours of the interview, remembering that your reason is that you are still trying to *sell* yourself.

Every interview should be followed up with a letter, not just a 'Thank you for seeing me' note, but one touching upon the main issues discussed at the interview and using the opportunity to refer to information which was given to you, showing that you absorbed it. A sample follow-up letter appears below. The letter must indicate your continuing interest in the job; use it to swing any decision in your favour. The company may be hesitating between you and someone else, and a letter might just tip the balance. (Obviously it will not affect an employer who has definitely made up his mind – either way – immediately after the interview.)

Letters which are not answered after ten days or so can be followed by a telephone call. You need only ask when you can

## After the Interview

**Sample follow-up letter to a company**

> 25 Oak Crescent,
> Anyville,
> Newtown,
> Midshire.
>
> 27 April 1988
>
> Mr R T Green,
> Managing Director,
> Bigtime Engineering PLC,
> Grease Street,
> Blackchester.
>
> Dear Mr Green,
>
> I very much enjoyed meeting you on Tuesday, and found our discussion of my background and its relevance to your requirements for the post of Engineering and Technical Manager in Bigtime Engineering most stimulating.
>
> Your company's expansion projects are most impressive and I was very interested to hear of your plans to enter new markets. I would like to confirm my interest in the appointment. As we discussed, my experience of managing the engineering function and adapting to new markets would help me to make an early contribution to your company's future developments.
>
> If you would like any further information about myself or my record I will be pleased to give it.
>
> I look forward to hearing from you.
>
> Yours sincerely,
>
>
> John W Smith

expect to hear of a decision; it may be that the firm has written to you but the letter has gone astray. Such persistence can do no harm and may improve your chance of success, as it is possible that a final decision has not been made; your continuing interest cannot do anything other than convince the company that yours is the name they should be writing into their plans.

When an application fails, job hunters tend to dispose of all material relating to the post. Should another vacancy appear with the same organization in the future, this leaves you with nothing on file; it is thus sensible to note the name of the firm, the person you saw, the job in question and the dates. Better still, keep copies of all the relevant correspondence and try to analyse why your application failed; this could help your presentation in the future.

I pointed out in chapter 6 that any verbal offer of employment made at interview should be countered with a request for time to consider the matter. Naturally you should also show interest in the prospect of an offer. However, the only safe course for any job hunter to follow is to await receipt of a written offer of employment before taking any irrevocable steps such as submitting your resignation from your current post.

When the written job offer arrives, only you with your family can make the decision: accept or decline? By now you will know as much as you are likely to learn about your prospective employer until you actually join the firm, you will have details of the full remuneration package and you will have an idea about the person to whom you would report. If you have any doubts, you can take twenty-four hours to think the decision through – you can always claim a postal delay if the firm telephones and tries to press for a response.

Should you decide to decline the offer, write to the company and thank it for its interest, explaining why you have decided to accept an alternative offer which more closely meets your career plans. Never be anything other than polite – you may find yourself applying to that company again in a few years' time for another position.

If the offer is one you really want and it matches your needs, telephone and accept it, telling the company that you will send written confirmation immediately. Take great care to make your acceptance unambiguous – do not let it appear to depend on the company's readiness to let you have a green car rather than a blue one or some equally trivial issue.

It is important to accept an employment offer by telephone and letter – all significant agreements should be subject to written confirmation for the sake of security. A phone call is essential because there is a slight chance that yours will be the letter which goes astray; after a few days the firm may conclude that you are not going to join it and withdraw the offer.

Some appointments will involve a service contract; if one is sent to you, reply by accepting the post but do not return the signed contract until it has been seen and approved by your solicitor. Usually contracts are to the advantage of the employee, but occasionally one might contain some clause which could restrict your future employment with a competitor. No reputable firm will demur at your action in referring the contract to your legal adviser – after all, the firm will have drawn it up with professional advice.

Every acceptance letter should include a sentence which says how much you look forward to taking up your new responsibilities, and you should clearly state the date you will join the company. You should also mention the main points in the company's offer letter – items such as salary, length of notice, holidays – along with any other important matters which have been discussed verbally.

Under the Employment Protection (Consolidation) Act, 1978, companies are legally required to issue written particulars of employment within thirteen weeks of engaging new staff. Minimum periods of notice and payment of staff under notice are also mandatory under the Act. The written particulars must cover:

1   identity of employee
2   identity of employer
3   starting date
4   whether service with a previous employer counts as continuous service with the present employer and, if so, the date on which the continuous period of employment began
5   rate of pay
6   interval of payment
7   hours of work
8   holiday entitlement and pay details

9   sickness and sick pay arrangements
10  job title
11  length of notice to be given and received
12  disciplinary rules
13  grievance procedure
14  disciplinary and appeals procedure
15  pensions and 'contracting out' arrangements.

Although the written particulars are not legally enforceable, like the Highway Code, courts and tribunals will take them into account at any hearing. Items 5 to 12 can be set out in various documents to which the employee may be referred but items 1 to 4 and 13 to 15 must be in a written statement. Employees do not have to sign a written statement although they may be asked to sign for *receipt* of a copy of the information.

Many of the points in the written particulars will form an important part of the offer and these are the ones which the offer letter should contain. Other details, while legally required, are less significant; if they are not included in the offer letter, check them before the end of your thirteenth week of employment.

That leaves the task of writing your letter of resignation to your present employer. This should give notice of your intention to leave on a given date, taking due note of your obligations to the company. As when you accept a new job, resignations should be given verbally and confirmed in writing. Your objective should always be to part company with your present employer on the best possible terms. If you ever find yourself dealing with the firm in future or meet up with former colleagues again, you want memories to be favourable on both sides, especially if you are likely to need references later.

The final step is to update your personal data bank – then it is all eyes to the future in the new post.

# 8
# Self-employed — or unemployed?

**SELF-EMPLOYMENT**

Particularly for the unemployed, self-employment can appear to have many attractions, especially if a large sum of redundancy money is available to help launch the venture. Many people have used this chance to do what they really want in life, going on to run pubs, post offices and so on. Many have prospered and found their true vocation; others have failed because they did not realize the demands of the business. Other ventures never get off the ground because the people who hope to run them choose to ignore market needs and set up to do what they want rather than ask themselves if anyone actually wants their product or service.

Another variation on this theme is to take on a franchise which allows an owner to run a business under the umbrella of a national name. This can be anything from a Wimpy bar to a travel agency or drain clearing service. For the payment of a fee, the expertise of the organization is made available and you receive considerable help to get things going. But beware of franchise opportunities. A number of these organizations appear to offer the moon and are in fact, little more than a confidence trick designed to part the recently redudant employee from his redundancy cheque. There is a franchise organization which exists to try and protect the name of genuine franchise operations and a call to them could prove worthwhile.

## Self-Employed — or Unemployed?

This book is not written with the intention of advising anyone who may be considering self-employment; there are plenty of specialist publications on the subject. One essential contact you should not overlook is the nearest branch of the Small Firms Service where considerable information and help is freely available. My only additional advice to readers is *take great care*. You could end up by losing all your redundancy money or other venture capital and miss out on the ideal appointment which was filled when you were thinking of other things.

### BUDGETS FOR UNEMPLOYMENT

The first thing anyone becoming unemployed must do is to register at the local Jobcentre. Unemployment benefit is only payable after you have 'signed on' and cannot be backdated, so make the Jobcentre your first call on your first day out of work.

People without jobs and incomes need to give careful thought to their financial commitments for the months ahead. As I have mentioned, to find a new job takes, on average, one month's searching for every £1,000 of salary expected. The higher the salary, the likelier it will be that this figure is exceeded, while job hunters at lower levels might hope to improve on the average. If your market is limited or particularly tight, you will have to expect a longer wait so the need for financial planning is great.

There should be four parts to your budget plan: your anticipated outgoings, your present cash reserves, income from odd sources and, finally, your assets which, if the going gets really rough, can be sold. Below are some model tables which can be used as the basis for your own financial plans.

### OUTGOINGS

Most people have their own special expenses in addition to the usual ones; add yours to the items on the list so that all

```
                                        MONTH
                            1 2 3 4 5 6 7 8 9 10 11 12

    Item
    Bills outstanding
    Debt interest
    Mortgage/rent
    Rates (incl. water)
    Electricity
    Gas
    Oil
    Coal
    Phone
    TV licence
    Insurance (life, house, effects)
    HP/TV rental
    Clubs/professional fees/
       subscriptions
    Car expenses (fuel, tax,
       maintenance, insurance)
    Public transport
    Children's lessons (swimming,
       music etc.)
    School meals
    Food
    Clothing
    Household goods
    Cosmetics/hairdresser
    Medical/dental bills
    Job search costs
    Other items


    TOTALS

    Add 10% contingency


    GRAND TOTALS
```

foreseeable expenditure is noted, and enter them monthly, quarterly or annually as appropriate.

## RESERVES

Add up your various reserves and divide them equally over the anticipated period of unemployment to show what the

# Self-employed — or unemployed?

```
                                    MONTH
                        1  2  3  4  5  6  7  8  9  10  11  12

Item

Current account
Deposit account
Savings accounts (building society,
   Post Office etc.)
Unit Trusts
Shares
Insurance policies
Piggy bank
Other sources                       _____

TOTALS                              _____
```

## INCOME

Again, fill in a table to help you plan ahead.

```
                                    MONTH
                        1  2  3  4  5  6  7  8  9  10  11  12

Item

Final pay
Holiday Pay
Redundancy money
Tax refunds
Interest from savings
Share dividends
Loans repaid to you
Spouse's pay
Children's contribution
   (if working and at home)
Part-time work
Consultancy work
Unemployment benefit/allowances
Letting an empty room               _____

TOTALS                              _____
```

average monthly figure could be if added to your expected income.

## SALEABLE ASSETS

All men and women who have worked for a few years in this country have paid their share of taxes and National Insurance contributions. The money they have paid goes in part to pay for benefits now available to them as unemployed persons. Newly unemployed people should therefore not be reluctant to collect the benefits of the insurance policy to which they have been contributing through the years.

However, the payout is small and will not go far, so, although no one wants to contemplate selling possessions which have been accumulated over many years, this prospect may have to be faced. It is not too difficult to start by clearing the items which have cluttered the loft for longer than anyone can recall, but if the situation worsens, some valued things may have to go too. The income from these items will not enter your calculations at first and there will be no regular monthly sum, although it may be useful to know the total value. Items to be considered for disposal include:

    second car
    boat/caravan
    unwanted bicycles
    jewellery
    music/hi-fi equipment
    stamp/coin collections
    paintings
    unwanted furniture/toys
    unwanted garden equipment
    holiday cottage.

Clearly life has become tough by the time this stage is reached, but you can delay such drastic steps by cutting back your outgoings from the earliest possible date. Unnecessary newspapers and magazines, fuel bills, expensive foods, gifts, video rentals and so on should all be curbed from the very beginning so that the remaining money stretches that bit further. It is easier to be strict at the start, when you and your family are suddenly aware of the change in circumstances, than to have to tighten the screw as time goes on, when the necessity may be less obvious to the younger members of the household. If a new job appears sooner than expected, your tight budgeting might mean that there can be a celebration with funds which had been earmarked for survival.

Your local Citizens' Advice Bureau will advise on the various kinds of help and benefits available or tell you where precise information can be obtained. Leaflets on benefits and other important matters can also be collected from Jobcentres. As the information is constantly changing, it is best to contact local CABs rather than rely on books and friends as the information both offer can quickly become out of date.

# 9
# From College to Career

No one would pretend that job hunting for college and university graduates is the simple task which it was in the 1960s. Then every graduate who qualified in the most obscure subject could still expect a selection of offers from many employers who recognized the degree as a sign of an ability to learn which could be utilized in many branches of industry and commerce. Today, with the pressures to trim labour forces, companies are cutting back on their intake of students as never before. Graduates must now learn to compete for the jobs which are available with the same vigour and determination as older job hunters who want to move on or who have become redundant. This chapter will show graduates how to face up to this challenge and improve their chances of being offered an opening.

**YOUTH AND MATURITY**

People who see their youth as a liability are simply saying that employers view their lack of experience as a drawback in relation to their salary and appointment objectives. Youth can, and must, be the easiest liability to turn into an advantage.

When composing your résumé or a letter, go out of your way to mention things like:

interest in a particular industry
drive
enthusiasm
ability to learn quickly
problem-solving talents
physical energy to devote to a task.

Naturally you will be short on work experience, but if you can point to some extra-curricular achievements, hobbies or part-time work, you will be able to project yourself as an interesting person worthy of an interview. Depending on their choice of career, some students can find work during their courses in suitable local firms on the odd afternoon, officially or otherwise, or during vacations.

If you are young, the key word is 'maturity'. You need to appear as down-to-earth, responsible and solid with evidence of ability to make sound judgements. Employers tend to shy away from candidates who show signs of eccentricity in appearance or behaviour and often settle on the safer choice of a 'conventional' type of applicant. You need to assess the employers in your chosen career and try to present yourself as the kind of applicant they feel at home with.

Youth can be a plus; immaturity is certainly a minus.

## WHAT CAREER?

Students are more fortunate than other job hunters in having a highly professional and successful careers guidance and advisory service provided specially for them.

Many people choose their lifelong jobs as a result of family influence which in most cases limits discussion to the kinds of work done by relatives and friends in the past, thereby excluding perhaps 95 per cent of the alternative ways of earning a living. Students have no such excuse and, at an early stage in your university or college careers, you should find out what information is available. There are books, leaflets and, most important, qualified people who will talk you through the possibilities as they relate to your interests and skills. Don't let your careers service just be a place where you pick up leaflets and handouts; make appointments with the advisers and press hard for help. Interest and effort from you will bring interest and effort from the adviser.

Time spent now in finding the right career will be time well spent. Too many people find themselves part-way through their working lives doing something they hate but trapped by their circumstances and unable to change course. Students can avoid this; if you are to profit from the services available to you, you must give this important issue your serious attention from your early college days.

Read through the reasons given for a move which are listed in chapter 2 under the heading 'Setting your sights'. These factors apply to the student as well as to the experienced job hunter: whether you like working with people rather than things, for example, is important in finding out where you should look for a career. Someone who is basically a 'loner' is unlikely to be happy in a sales or marketing job, and an employer is equally unlikely to be overjoyed with his or her performance in that type of work. Quite quickly, that wrong combination would lead to disaster.

Graduates must think about their values – people or things, thinking or doing, ambitious or desirous of security, risk-taker or cautious, regular hours in a fixed location or work any time and any place, leader or follower. Your involvement in clubs, societies and sports and whether you held office or merely took part all indicate the personality traits which help point to a career.

Career guidance is not a question of spending a quick five minutes reading through a few leaflets, but requires the benefit of trained expertise which is available to everyone to some extent but particularly to students through their advisory services. Only when students have considered their basic choices should they begin to narrow their search for likely employers in the chosen field. Being sure that you have selected your career intelligently is a certain way to build self-confidence which the perceptive interviewer will pick up, and that, in turn, is likely to bring more job offers.

## FINDING AN EMPLOYER

Having decided on their chosen career, all students must make full use of the services available in each college and university which bring together companies and students. By far the best known initial contact with employers is on the 'milk round', the flippant title given to the three-month travelling circus of employer-representatives who journey around the colleges in an annual effort to find the pick of the graduate crop for their companies. Theirs is the difficult task of seeing perhaps hundreds of students and trying to decide who will be amongst the 10 per cent or so worth a more detailed interview in the Easter vacation, probably on the firm's premises.

Usually you get on the interview list by completing application forms for the companies which interest you (either their own form or the standard one from the careers service) and returning them directly to the firms or through the careers adviser. In the same way that application forms for later jobs must be completed with care, attention to detail is also important for graduates, and the points noted in chapter 4 should be carefully considered. With a very great number of applicants from which to choose, companies will be looking for ways of thinning out the aspiring trainees. Any badly presented applications will be destined for rejection.

The meagre half-hour interview which will result from a good application form may seem very short and insignificant to you, but as far as the company is concerned it has to be multiplied by many hundreds, and so your effort to show that you merit that small slice of time begins when you put pen to paper. It is an opportunity which must not be wasted.

Inevitably, some graduates will be unsuccessful on the milk round or will prefer to apply to firms which do not visit colleges; their search for employment will continue later in the year. Help is still available from the careers service and if you attended a college some distance away and are now at home, you are entitled to make use of the facilities at your nearest university or college, thus saving travel or postage. In addition, you will need to step up your own efforts which might involve letters, résumés and application forms; see the samples below for ideas. Incidentally, the tital 'Personal history' is more appropriate than 'Career history' for a graduate whose career has not yet begun. It will pay to develop two or three slightly different personal histories for use with different types of organization or industry, although there is no need to consider a completely separate one for every application as you will probably be applying for graduate training appointments in each case.

## THE APPLICATION FORM GAME

First, carefully re-read chapter 4. Obviously students will not have previous full-time work experience (the mature student is an exception dealt with below), so it is important to state academic qualifications and grades in full.

Application forms must be completed neatly and legibly, contain no spelling or grammatical errors and be relevant to the post and company in question. Anything else means your application is heading for the biggest pile of all – the rejections – and you are one step nearer the dole queue. Remember that application forms are a means of rejecting people, not selecting them.

Whatever your view of the older generation and its standards, this is not the time to show your feelings by failing to comply with expected norms of presentation. Play the game

## Historical style résumé for a graduate

<u>PERSONAL HISTORY</u>

Helen Margaret JONES, 14 Elm Drive, Suburbia, Southshire
Tel: Suburbia (0123) 45678
Term Address: Flat 4, New Hall, University Ave., Castletown

| | |
|---|---|
| OBJECTIVE | A graduate trainee appointment in the packaging industry where my Business Studies degree and experience of part-time work can contribute to the organization. |
| DATE OF BIRTH | January 16 1967 |
| PERSONAL | Single, height 5'6", weight 9st, in excellent health. British citizen. Clean driving licence. |
| EDUCATION | 1978-80 Blacktown Grammar School, Blacktown |
| | 1980-84 Glasswall Comprehensive School, Suburbia |
| | 1984-88 Ivory Towers University, Castletown |
| QUALIFICATIONS | O levels in Biology (B), Eng. Lang. (C), Eng.Lit.(B), French (C), Geog.(D), Hist.(B), Maths (B), Physics (B) |
| | A levels in Economics (B), English (C), History (B) |
| | B.A. (Business Studies), Second Class Honours, 1983 |
| WORK EXPERIENCE | |
| 1982 | Weekend work at Lowpryce Stores, responsible for filling shelves and reporting stock levels. |
| 1982 - 1983 | Weekend work at Hyclass Superstores, responsible for four students in three departments, maintaining full shelves. Also occasional checkout duties on relief basis. |
| 1983 - 1984 | Weekend work in Smalltrees Departmental Emporium as sales assistant in hi-fi and video department. |
| INTERESTS | At school, I was a regular member of the squash team and president of the debating society. In my final year, I was appointed school Vice-Captain. |
| | I am Social Secretary of the Explorers' Club at University and my duties include organizing social events and field trips to all parts of the country. This involves liaison with hotel staff and local naturalists. |
| | At University I play squash and am a member of the Car Club which exists to give mutual aid to students who are car owners. |
| | Between completing my finals and starting on my training, I hope to find work overseas. |

according to the rules. If you don't like the rules, wait until you are in before you try to change them — if you still want to by then — or choose a career where conventions are not

## Sample cover letter for a speculative c.v. from a graduate to a company

> 14 Elm Drive,
> Suburbia,
> Southshire.
>
> 19 May 1988
>
> Mr L S White,
> Personnel and Training Manager,
> Breakapart Packaging PLC,
> Greenfields Industrial Estate,
> Lowtown,
> Swampshire.
>
> Dear Mr White,
>
> As a company which annually recruits a number of new graduates, you may have a vacancy for someone with a Business Studies degree, and I would appreciate it if you would consider me as a candidate.
>
> I am particularly interested in joining your organization as I have had some part-time experience of the problems and economics of packaging when working with local retailers over the past three years. This showed me that the packaging and presentation of a product has a significant influence on its success in the market as well as on its profitability.
>
> My Business Studies course has given me additional knowledge of the economics of manufacture, and I believe that my practical and theoretical training will quickly allow me to contribute to your firm if I am offered a place.
>
> I enclose a copy of my personal history and I hope my qualifications and experience will earn me a place on you shortlist of graduates for interview this year.
>
> I look forward to hearing from you.
>
> Yours sincerely,
>
> Helen M Jones

important and which is predominantly 'young' in outlook.

The demands on your concentration made by application forms may be tiresome and boring, but they cannot be sidestepped. So learn to type well or, if this is not practical, practise a clear style of printing. Even the most stylish handwriting, if illegible, does little to convince the firm that you are thinking of their needs, and if they are obliged to try and decipher the high-speed scribble you used in lectures they will not be impressed.

Read the questions very carefully and plan your answers to make the best use of the available space. Most forms invite you to use plain paper if you cannot fit everything in, but the recipients will not welcome the extra demands on their time and concentration if you write an essay on each point. It is best to write out your answers on a separate sheet of paper and show them to a friend before commiting them to the official form. This will often expose gaps and help you tighten up the wording. As recommended for experienced job hunters, you may find it helpful to photocopy the application form and complete the copy for practice.

The danger areas coincide with the opportunities to sell yourself effectively. They usually arise in the sections headed 'Additional information' or 'Interests and activities'. Thoughtful students who want to be successful job hunters will complete these sections with carefully worded material which relates to the job and the firm. They will take the chance of not only stating their interest in social activities and sport, but expanding this into:

> I am a regular member of my college tennis/hockey/football/squash team and for the past year I have been social secretary of the Explorers' Club, responsible for organizing social events and field trips all over the country for groups of twenty to thirty people, involving liaison with hostel and hotel staff and naturalists.

This makes it clear that the firm is looking at someone who shows signs of leadership, can be a good team member and has organizing ability.

Any vacation or part-time work should be mentioned; stress any additional responsibilities you had beyond the normal duties. Naturally you should highlight any experience related to the kind of job you are seeking.

The point to be stressed is that you must seize every chance to project yourself rather than let the application appear to be just one of many with nothing special to commend it. At the same time, there should be no hint that you have filled space with waffle just to avoid blanks. *Think hard* about what you have done that makes you different and will catch the eye of the employer.

An accompanying letter must be securely attached to every application form; a sample is shown below.

**Sample cover letter for an application form from a graduate**

```
                                        14 Elm Drive,
                                        Suburbia,
                                        Southshire.

                                        19 May 1988



Mr L S White,
Personnel and Training Manager,
Breakapart Packaging PLC,
Greenfields Industrial Estate,
Lowtown,
Swampshire.




Dear Mr White,

I am pleased to enclose my application form for the post of
graduate trainee.

I am particularly interested in joining your organization as
I have had some part-time experience of the problems and economies
of packaging when working with local retailers over the past
three years. This showed me that the packaging and presentation
of a product has a significant influence on its success in
the market as well as on its profitability.

My Business Studies course has given me additional knowledge
of the economics of manufacture, and I believe that my practical
and theorectical training will quickly allow me to contribute
to your firm if I am offered a place.

I hope you will find my qualifications and experience of interest,
and I look forward to hearing from you.

Yours sincerely,




       Helen M Jones
```

## PREPARATION FOR INTERVIEW

If your application has won you an invitation to an interview on the milk round, research is needed into the company as with any other interview. Here graduates score over other job hunters by having at their disposal a vast amount of easily accessible information at the careers office; this must now be investigated. For a milk round interview, the details you need to search out will be relatively easy to find. It is essential that applicants know the products and services of the company they hope to join, the number of staff it employs and where they are based, together with as much information as they can obtain about their own particular area of interest within the company. Interviewers are only too pleased to discover that students have made some effort to anticipate the obvious questions and they expect more than empty clichés when they ask the inevitable 'Why have you chosen this type of career?', followed by 'What makes you want to join our company?'

Of course, if you have friends or relatives who work in your chosen field or company, make sure that you get from them some information which you can use at the interview to show that you are better informed and keener than most to join the firm. Such knowledge makes you stand out from the crowd and will go a long way to persuading the weary interviewer that you are someone the company must look at twice – which is exactly the reason why you took care with the application form and your pre-interview research.

Possible questions for students to put to their interviewers might include what has happened to previous student intakes and how the training is planned and, equally important, assessed. Some years ago, 'training' consisted of a prolonged tour of all the departments in a company, with trainees spending weeks or months in each but with no clear objectives. This model has mostly been superseded by proper training programmes, but students should try to discover something about the company's plans to avoid the risk of a time-wasting, second-rate introduction to working life.

If 'acceptable' appearance and punctuality are important for the experienced job hunter, they are doubly so for the graduate. There is simply no possibility that a company, faced with an abundance of riches from which to choose, is going to select a candidate who turns up late and is dressed in an eccentric style. Companies want to see if students can look the part when necessary, and being well turned out shows that, if nothing else, you have a sense of what is appropriate. Good grooming means neat hair, clean hands and clean, neat clothing. For jobs in the media, advertising and other 'glamorous' professions, fashionable, individual clothing is an asset; for the rest of the business world, avoid dress which might be interpreted as flashy or unconventional. If narrow ties are fashionable, a 'shoestring' tie would be taking things further than is prudent. Women students will no longer raise eyebrows by appearing in trousers, but don't venture into extremes of fashion. Your interviewer may be an old fuddy-duddy deeply suspicious of anything remotely construable as 'trendy'. A person's attitudes are often thought to be reflected by their appearance, and as this is part of your personal presentation, it must be of as high a standard as possible. Denim is not seen by the business community as acceptable dress.

## THE INTERVIEW

Again, re-read the advice on interviews in chapter 6. For students, one difference in the first interview is that the milk round interviewers are likely to include some staff who are not from the personnel department, but are managers from other parts of the company. They will be less familiar with interview techniques and will probably do their job by going through the application form and asking about the areas which most interest them.

Once again, answers must be given in a way which displays your talents and achievements. In the short time available, it is up to you to give your interviewers the information they are seeking in a positive way, rather than just uttering monosyllabic replies.

It is essential to remember that however bad, incompetent, uninterested or old-fashioned these people may appear to be, they hold the key to your hopes of progress to the next stage. If you want to get that far, you will have to get on with the interviewers facing you – as you will when they are your colleagues. Think of their feelings. They are probably stuck in some cell of a room for a week, facing the prospect of seeing ten to twelve students per day. Most of the students' faces will be a blur in their memories – except yours. You are going to impress them as someone different, first by the way you have already presented your application form and letter and now by your skills at selling yourself more effectively than your colleagues. By the end of the interview, you are going to be remembered and, who knows, well on the way into the firm.

The successful student job hunter will, as a result of a good first interview, be invited to a second meeting with the employer, probably on company premises during the Easter vacation. Additional preparation is now needed: look back over the advice given in the earlier part of the book and refresh your mind about the facts you have already gathered. You will have been given some new information at your first interview – review it now, ready for bringing out at the second interview to show that you did listen to what was said.

The second interview will almost certainly involve a walk around the firm's premises, when you may well be escorted by someone who will not actually interview you but who will certainly be asked to report on how you responded to what you saw and whom you met. Careful listening, thoughtful questions and a polite response to people you meet are obviously essential. Even apparently casual talk about the weather, interests and life in general is an important way for the firm to find out something about the type of person you are. Your objective is to appear as a rounded, sociable individual who knows how to respond to others without antagonizing them or being anything other than an intelligent and pleasant potential colleague. The more formal part of the interview should be handled with the same attention to self-presentation as recommended in chapter 7.

Many interviewers may seem, correctly or not, to be condescending to students. In turn, many students appear arrogant and immature to their interviewers. As an interviewee, you should be aware of the image each side has of the other and make a strenuous effort to avoid conforming to unfavourable stereotypes. You cannot do much about altering interviewers' prejudices permanently but you can ensure that they do not see you as confirming their view. Show that you have your feet firmly on the ground and that no one could accuse you of arrogance – an unpleasant characteristic at any level or age. Young people often believe that they can do things better than their seniors and they may be right! The odd thing is that students have always thought that, but when their turn to be the 'older generation' comes, they are equally criticized by the new youth.

At interview, avoid the extremes of superciliousness and subservience; promote the impression of a well-balanced, moderate individual who will easily and happily fit into a company and contribute to its success.

It is unlikely that a graduate will be able to improve on the fixed pay scale which the company will have for new recruits, and there is no future in arguing the point unless you want to lose any job which may be offered.

### Group interviews

Students may also find themselves part of a group all invited to attend a second interview at the same time; the company has little chance of doing things otherwise if it plans to see a large number of candidates during the short Easter holiday. This arrangement raises the possibility of an additional method of selection – the group discussion.

At a group discussion, the candidates are usually seated around a table. A member of the firm's staff will brief them, probably telling them that they will be given a topic to discuss. He or she may ask the group to reach its conclusions within a fixed time period, and will point out that members of the company will observe the group but will not participate in the discussions. The topic will be announced and the observers will play no further part in the proceedings other than to watch.

Group discussions can be difficult from a number of viewpoints. If any order is to prevail and any conclusions are to be reached, the group must organize itself. That means that it needs someone to control it – a chairman or chairwoman – and the first step is for the group to appoint someone from within its ranks. If you are tempted to volunteer, resist unless you have some experience of the task. A poor chairman will not secure the respect of the group and will be unable to contribute freely to the discussion – a loser twice over. However, if you have the skills that are required, offer to do the job, and doing it well will make you stand out.

As a group member, you must be seen to contribute. Offer balanced comments, putting both sides of the case before saying where you stand. Careful listening will also be noted by the observers and needless to say you should display courtesy to the other members of the group, building on the points they make and never trying to shout them down. Your remarks should be addressed to the chair and you should never attempt to score off others with cheap debating points. Your objective should be to appear as a contributor of positive points which help lead the group towards its conclusion, making contributions which are neither too brief nor excessively long.

## THE MATURE STUDENT

For some years now, there has been an increase in the number of people taking higher education courses a few years after having left school instead of the more usual procedure of going straight from school to college or university. The resultant 'mature students' will, course over, find some differences in the way employers look at them compared to their younger counterparts.

Some firms can find it difficult to accommodate someone who might be ten or more years older than the usual graduate intake, but there are others which welcome a recruit who has more experience of life. The welcome is coupled with higher hopes and older students should make the most of the knowledge which their younger colleagues lack. Students who have already held a number of jobs will be able to point to responsibilities they have carried and possibly staff they have controlled. Such skills already in evidence can be particularly attractive to an employer and should certainly be highlighted in an application form or résumé.

Mature women students are often seen as useful recruits, especially if they have qualified and are returning to work after having had a family. Employers may conclude that they have taken an objective view of their role in the family and have chosen a career deliberately after years of thought. There are unlikely to be other career interruptions for such women, and the level headedness they bring to a job will make them attractive candidates in many firms and types of work.

Older graduates need to put in more effort with their application forms and résumés to avoid having them discarded on account of age. Pay particular attention to using interesting words to select and describe those parts of your experience which show that you have something special to offer. Previous work experience and responsibility, offices held in voluntary organizations, evidence of having put down roots making you unlikely to move within a year or so – all these help to sell your attributes and take the spotlight away from your date of birth.

As a mature graduate you will have to steel yourself for a low rate of pay geared to the more usual age range of students. Until you are employed and trained, the company is unlikely to think that you will bring much more value to the job, although your maturity may improve the offer slightly. However, once you are working it should be possible to move up the scale faster than others and be in a stronger position to gain early promotion.

## SETTLING IN

Even in the best organization, settling in is not an easy time. New recruits ought to find properly drawn up induction training programmes awaiting them but, for the best reasons in the world, things seldom go according to plan. People who should be taking your under their wing for a day or a week or two suddenly find that they have to cover for a colleague who is off ill, and so improvisation takes over.

Under any circumstances, newcomers will attract favourable attention by taking initiative – seeking out company literature, talking to colleagues and observing how they do their jobs, being ready to assist with the most mundane task. A willingness to roll up your sleeves and complete some urgent job will show that you are ready to plug a gap and will encourage others to accept you as a member of the team. It is a good idea to make notes on the routine tasks you are shown, as people grow tired of having to explain things more than once.

Graduates also have to learn to fit into the disciplines of working life. There will usually be fixed hours of work and as these will be observed by everyone from the managing director downwards, it will be difficult for you to plead a special case on the grounds that you are not at your best until midday! You might discover for the first time that some people will resent your qualifications; you will need to put in a lot of effort to win their confidence and achieve a good working relationship with them. Perhaps you will discover for the first time that not everyone can match your intellectual level, and you will need to adapt to this very quickly unless you want to be regarded as an unapproachable egghead.

In the early weeks of postgraduate employment, new recruits may find themselves underworked or doing tasks which any trained monkey could do. Both situations can rapidly lead to frustration and deep disappointment. The problem may stem from the firm's lack of previous experience in employing graduates and the solution is to complete the tasks which have been set, then try to discuss the situation with someone who can alter your position. Graduates who refuse to do some everyday jobs stand to make themselves look foolish when in most firms senior staff will do whatever is needed to get work out and keep customers happy. Moreover, graduates in the present circumstances are often filling jobs previously done by less well-qualified people as opportunities at higher levels are fewer than before.

If the problem of underemployment persists and your efforts to improve the position bring no improvement, it may be necessary to look elsewhere for a job and put it all down to experience. In that situation, turn back to the beginning of this book and work through the processes which lead to success in job hunting.

# 10
# Action Plan

Everyone's job hunt is unique from the point of view of career objectives, opportunities and possible alternatives. But whatever your background, a clear action plan is of the utmost help and the summary below covers the main things to be done. Circumstances will dictate the order of events in individual cases; many of them will proceed in parallel with others.

- Think through your own strengths and weaknesses.
- Consider your personal job likes and dislikes.
- Identify your own job satisfaction needs.
- Pinpoint your industry and career possibilities.
- Determine your income and responsibility goals.
- Learn about the skills and techniques of job changing.
- Plan how you are going to market yourself and set timescales.
- Build your personal data bank.
- Consider the various résumé styles available.
- Choose your preferred style.
- Draft, redraft and redraft again your career history until it is absolutely right.
- Set up your typing arrangements.
- Produce your résumé using your chosen paper.
- Have 20 copies made of the résumé, supplying your own paper.

Rewrite the résumé to suit specific jobs as required.
Draft standard letter for speculative applications.
Prepare rough drafts of standard letters for answering advertisements.
Prepare rough drafts of standard cover letters to accompany résumés and application forms.
Prepare lists of your personal contacts.
Prepare lists of employment agencies, possible firms, trade shows, etc.
Prepare lists of personal, social and business contacts to be cultivated.
Check with your referees.
Check on availability (where and when) of trade journals.
Read books on psychological testing and other relevant topics (see the list of useful Publications and Addresses).
Send out your speculative letters.
Watch the newspaper advertisements.
Write items for publication in trade journals.
Follow up unanswered letters and contacts.
Consider the possibility of self-advertising.
At intervals, rehash your résumé in the light of experience.
Set up a record system and keep it straight.

## A LAST WORD

Finding a good new job is hard work. It requires creativity, patience and resilience. It is particularly hard to provide all these qualities if you are redundant and jobs in your line are few and far between. The odds against can seem very long ones.

The disappointment when an application fails is even greater when, as can happen, the potential employer telephones you between the first and second interview – action which can only be interpreted as showing interest and which is bound to raise your hopes of success. If at the final interview, encouraging comments are made, and all seems to go well, it appears that the promised telephone call will merely be a formality to confirm the offer of appointment. When the call does not materialize within twenty-four hours, the real situation becomes apparent and self-doubt reasserts itself. It is not easy to watch the postman call and go to the door to collect your letter, only to find that it confirms your worst fears. A thin envelope tells its own tale when you were hoping for a fat one with its file of papers setting out details of that much-desired new job.

When a final decision goes against you, especially when the job looked tailor-made, it is bound to be a setback, but the successful job hunter will win through sooner than most, often to an even better job. Use the experience positively; next time, discipline yourself not to build your hopes until you hold the offer in your hands. Never, however unfair, unjust or unethical you may consider the selection system to have been, write and complain. It will not change the company's decision; it will confirm your unsuitability in the hirer's mind, and it will cost you a stamp. That company's loss is the next firm's gain.

Individuals can succeed even in the toughest situation, but it is less of a strain if job hunting is a team job involving your whole family. After all, it may be the job hunter who is the focus of activity, but the whole family's future is often at stake, where you are the bread-winner. Job hunting is a team game − a single person competing against other teams will have to work extra hard, but someone who is part of a family yet does not have their support is in for a particularly tough time. Successful job hunters need loyalty and mutual support.

For job hunters who value their career, investment of time and money in their own future will help them make the most of the rest of their own and their family's lives. It is a demanding and exciting task in which the rewards match the effort. Good luck and happy job hunting!

# The Seven Point Plan

The Seven Point Plan is a commonly used framework for assessing job applicants at interviews. It was developed by Alec Rodger and published in 1952, and although no plan can give a guarantee of success in interviewing, its use ensures that the interviewer takes an organised look at the candidate. I give a brief summary here:

1  *Physical*. Does the applicant have the necessary physical attributes for the job? These might include height, weight, strength, vision, ability to withstand heat, cold, working indoors or outdoors. Is the person's appearance satisfactory and voice suitable for the job in question?
2  *Attainments*. What educational qualifications or work experience does the job holder need?
3  *General intelligence*. How much general intelligence does the job require? How quick on the uptake does the person have to be? Is the applicant over-intelligent for the job, which will lead to dissatisfaction on both sides?
4  *Special aptitudes*. Does the job call for any special abilities such as ability to draw or write well? Is a talent in music or numeracy needed? Special aptitudes are particularly important when selecting someone who may not be highly intelligent but has a marked skill which can be harnessed in certain types of work.

5   *Interests*. Can the applicant demonstrate some particular interest which is specially useful in the job? Is a practical, artistic, social or intellectual interest desirable in the successful applicant?
6   *Disposition*. Does the job require the person to be specially self-reliant, cheerful, strong-willed, persuasive and so on?
7   *Circumstances*. Does the job call for any particular time or financial sacrifices? Does it require the person to be away from home a lot? Is the personal background likely to have a bearing on the ability of the candidate to do the job well?

The Seven Point Plan does not do anything by itself – it is only a way of classifying information and there is no obligation on its user to take the headings in any special order. It is the interviewer's guide, and if it is being used, you know you are being interviewed by someone who is at least trying to be professional.

# Useful Addresses and Publications

British Franchise Association,
Franchise Chambers,
75A Bell Street,
Henley-on-Thames,
Oxon RG9 2BD.

City Business Library,
Gillett House,
55 Basinghall Street,
London EC2V 5BX.

Company information of all types.

Companies House,
Crown Way,
Cardiff.

Records on limited companies.

Executive Reserve Manpower Services Ltd.,
Templar House,
81/87 High Holborn,
London WC1V 6NP.

Brings together companies and qualified people for short-term employment.

Executive Standby,
310 Chester Road,
Hartford,
Northwich,
Cheshire CW8 2AB;

60, Beaks Hill,
King's Norton,
Birmingham B38 8BY;

37/39 Victoria Road,
Darlington,
Co. Durham.

Brings together companies and qualified people for short-term employment.

Small Firms Service

Exists to give advice to all small companies in or about to start a business. Offices throughout the UK. Contact on Freefone 2444.

*Directory of Opportunities for Graduates*

published annually by VNU Business Publications. Information on companies which recruit graduates.

*Executive Post*

Weekly newspaper available through PER carrying advertisements for vacancies notified to PER.

*Graduate Opportunities*

published annually by New Opportunity Press. Information on companies which recruit graduates.

*Graduate Post*

Fortnightly newspaper available through PER and Careers Advisory Service to graduates.

## Useful Publications and Addresses

*How to be Interviewed*

by D. Mackenzie Davey and P. McDonnell (British Institute of Management, 1980).
A brief guide on basic interview technique.

*Opportunities*

Weekly newspaper for local authority vacancies. Available in libraries.

*Personnel and Training Management Yearbook*

published annually by Kogan Page.
Lists organizations, directors and area in which they operate within personnel and consultancy fields.

*Selection and Assessment at Work*

by G. Jessop and H. Jessop (Methuen, 1975).
Aptitude and psychology tests.

*The Seven Point Plan*

by Alec Rodger (NFER Publishing Company, 1952).
A brief description of selection interviewing using the Seven Point Plan.

*Women's Rights: A Practical Guide*

by A. Coote and T. Gill (Penguin, 1981).
A guide to the workings of the law concerning discrimination against women.

*Working at Home for Profit*

by J. Johnson (Blackwell, 1980).
A guide to home employment.

*Working for Yourself*

by G. Golzen (Kogan Page, 1981).
Step by step guide to self-employment.

# Index

Advertisements, 34–40, 47–8
Age, 15–17, 69, 104–5, 118–19
Agencies, 41–3
Appearance, 61–3, 114
Application forms, 49–52, 108–12
Aptitude tests, 53–6

Box numbers, 43

Care of children, 72
Career counselling, 43
Career history,
   functional style, 25, 28
   graduate, 109
   historical style, 25, 27
   layout, 23–4
   obituary style, 9, 25, 26
   presentation, 22–3, 29
   writers, 24
Closing techniques, 83–5
Company research, 57–9
Consultancies, 41–3
Contracts, 96–7
Curriculum vitae – *see* Career history

Data bank, 17–21
Direct approach, 44–7
Dress, 61–3

Employment agencies, 41–3
Ending the interview, 83–5

Feedback from interview, 84
Financial planning, 99-103

Graduate job hunter,
   advantage of youth, 104–5
   application forms, 108–12
   choice of careers, 105–7
   finding employers, 107–8
   interview preparation, 113–14
   interviews, 114–17
   personal history, 109

Handwriting tests, 52–3
Headhunters, 47
Hobbies, 49, 68

Informal chat, 87–8
Interests, 50, 68
Interviews,
   appearance, 61–3
   closing techniques, 83–5
   dos and don'ts, 76–80
   graduate interviews, 114–17
   preparation, 57–73, 113–14
   problems for women, 70–3
   punctuality, 63–4
   questions to answer, 64–9
   questions to ask, 59–60
   timing, 61

## Index

Interview types,
  informal chat, 87–8
  panel, 89–90
  stress, 88

Job Clubs, 14–15
Job hopper, 25
Job objectives, 11
Job offers,
  accepting, 95–6
  declining, 95
Job sources,
  agencies, 41–3
  box numbers, 43
  direct approach, 44–7
  head hunters, 47
  PER, 40–1
  personal contacts, 31
  press reports, 34
  self-advertising, 47–8
  situations vacant, 35–40
  social and public bodies, 32
  trade shows, 33–4

Leisure interests, 50, 68
Length of service, 69
Letters,
  c.v. or application form cover, 39, 42
  follow up, 94
  replies to advertisements, 38
  speculative, 35

Male chauvinism, 70–1
Marital status, 71–2
Mature students, 118–19
Money, 50, 68–9, 80–3
Moving on, 5–6

Negotiating on salary, 80–3

Objectives, 4–5, 11
Older job hunters, 16–17

Panel interview, 89–90
PER, 13, 40–1
Personal data bank, 17–21

Personal history, *see* Career history
Post-interview action, 93–7
Psychological tests, 53–6
Punctuality, 61

Questions to answer, 64–9, 113
Questions to ask, 59–60

Records, 94–5
Redundancy, 69, *see also* Unemployed
References, 50, 90–1
Registers, 41–3
Research, 57–9
Résumé, *see* Career history
Retraining, 12

Salary, 50, 68–9, 80–3
Self-advertising, 47–8
Self employment, 98
Service contract, 96–7
Seven Point Plan, 78, 124–5
Sexual innuendo, 71
Stress interview, 88

Telephone Interviews, 85–7
Tests, 52–6
Time of interview, 61
Timing the response, 44
Trade shows, 33–4

Unemployed,
  action to take, 99–103
  budgets, 99–103
  dilemma, 12–17
  lower paid job, 13
  older person, 16–17
  temporary post, 13

Women, special problems 70–3
Work objectives, 4–5, 11

Youth problems, 104–5